GLOBAL TERRORISM

Challenges and Policy Options

GLOBAL TERRORISM

Challenges and Policy Options

Editors

Dhruv C. Katoch

Shakti Sinha

INDIA FOUNDATION
ANALYSIS | ADVOCACY | AWARENESS

PENTAGON PRESS

Global Terrorism: Challenges and Policy Options
A Compendium of Issues Discussed at the Second Jaipur Counter Terrorism Conference: 2016, under the aegis of The Government of Rajasthan and India Foundation, 02-03 February 2016

Editors: Dhruv C. Katoch and Shakti Sinha

First Published in 2017

ISBN 978-81-8274-950-4

Published by
PENTAGON PRESS
206, Peacock Lane, Shahpur Jat
New Delhi-110049
Phones: 011-64706243, 26491568
Telefax: 011-26490600
email: rajan@pentagonpress.in
website: www.pentagonpress.in

Printed at Aegean Offset Printers, Greater Noida, U.P.

Contents

PART II
CONTESTING THE SCOURGE

Introduction

Shakti Sinha

One of our contributors very aptly questions the belief that terrorism is difficult to understand; rather, it is definitely the most *intentionally* misunderstood phenomenon. This is because while countries notionally sign up to the idea that 'one man's terrorist cannot be another man's freedom fighter', the reality is that all states have their strategic priorities and that in many cases they have themselves nurtured either the conditions that gave rise to terrorism or actually created the terrorist groups whose blowback actions they are now facing. It is this that complicates tackling terrorism—not the understanding of what it is.

Global Terrorism: Challenges and Policy Options arose out of the proceedings of the second Counter Terrorism Conference organised at Jaipur (February 2-3, 2016). It was inaugurated by Shri Pranab Mukherjee, the Honourable President of India, and saw ministerial interventions from Afghanistan, India, Bangladesh, Malaysia and Iran. The various sessions saw experts from all over the world present the security, financial, political and military perspectives, from the universal to the contextual. These different perspectives did not conform to any grand master plan and are occasionally at odds with each other, which brings variety and lets the readers decide for themselves as what seems to be the most convincing.

This introduction will not attempt to be a summary of the book, since that would not do justice to the richness of the arguments put forth by the different contributors. The attempt instead is to draw attention to a few key issues, some of which come up repeatedly in different articles. Hopefully, this would whet the appetite of the reader, who would want to get into the nitty-gritty of the specific issue.

The first such issue is that terrorism is not an ideology but a tactic—a method of achieving political goals. The Left-wing extremists indiscriminately liquidated 'class enemies', while ethnic nationalists like the LTTE used suicide bombers very extensively. The Daesh's brutality came as a shocker to the Western world since the killings, abductions, rapes, etc. were published by the perpetrators themselves very effectively. But the Daesh was hardly the first Islamic extremist group using terror; the Taliban's mass murder of Shias (Hazaras) after the capture of Mazar-i-Sharif, the destruction of the Bamiyan Buddhas and scorched earth policy in the Shomali plains never got traction in the West as the Daesh's atrocities have, though the parallel is striking. The reasons why the Daesh's actions were viewed with so much horror in addition to the publicity it itself generated was the sheer public brutality and audaciousness (public beheading, burning a victim in his cage, mass rapes and public justification for female slavery, blowing up Greek-era monuments that the people in the West could identify with, etc.) that such brutality could actually draw in recruits globally, and that so many of the recruits come from Europe and not from desperately poor countries in Asia and Africa. In the bargain, the policymakers and analysts feel paralysed and start looking at the bigger picture – how to tackle terrorism as a phenomenon? While such philosophical efforts should not be belittled if we are to create a world where the recourse to violence is stigmatised, and punished, and individual causes that the terrorists exploit addressed, the requirement to physically eliminate the physical force that is at the heart of each terrorist group cannot be lost sight of.

The second issue, noted earlier, is that many countries continue to patronise terrorist outfits as the people of India and Afghanistan know so well, being at the receiving end. Also, since many of the terrorist groups have either had past dealings with individual superpowers, or arose as a consequence of a failed intervention, there is a lack of honesty in dealing with such groups. So hopes for a global compact that would bring an end to state support for terrorism, and to the ecosystem that allows the funding, financing and support to terrorists groups, are not likely to materialise. This then has two implications. The first is that at the regional level, countries must cooperate more closely. Though South Asia is seen as the least integrated and most disjointed region, its countries have developed remarkably effective bilateral and larger cooperative mechanisms. These include security cooperation and the sharing of intelligence; the benefits have been denial of sanctuaries and the handing over of terrorists to the countries where they are accused of many crimes. India has signed Mutual Legal Assistance Treaties with Afghanistan, Bangladesh and Sri Lanka. Similarly, the sharing of intelligence with the US, Europe, Saudi Arabia and others has increased and become more effective. The other implication is that the efforts at naming and shaming should intensify, so that a critical mass of support can be achieved that would lead to the adoption of universal norms necessary to tackle terrorism. In the meantime, participation in forums like the Financial Action Task Force should continue and be deepened, with a failure to act by the specific countries being highlighted. International cooperation is necessary to prevent the use not just of cross-border financial flows, but for example, the procurement of arms and ammunitions that sustain the terrorist groups. Sri Lanka's success in denying oxygen to the LTTE is commendable but would come out a cropper if a neighbouring country were to give sanctuary, and arm a terrorist group, as Afghanistan has found out in the resurgence of the Taliban. Therefore, international cooperation has to be made more effective. Fortunately, past successes in outlawing chemical weapons, for example, demonstrate that many 'impossibly unrealistic' aims can get universal support.

The third set of issues deal with the radicalisation of Islam, particular among the youth. Experience has shown that the elimination of one terrorist group often means that it gets replaced by another or has a re-emergence in a more virulent form, as the Taliban did post-2004. The seeming endless flow of recruits, particularly from the educated, internet-savvy youth including females, for the cause of the jihad, has to be staunched.

De-radicalisation has worked in different countries, but the greater acceptance of Wahhabi/Salafi thinking among the Muslim communities worldwide poses a particularly intractable obstacle. Obviously, its continued funding would ensure that the theological ecosystem of supremacist beliefs and xenophobia necessary for radicalisation is still in place though individual groups like the Daesh may be losing flavour. It has been argued that the so-called moderate voices opposing the Daesh's, and other similar extremism end up supporting the legitimisation of such thinking as they do not offer an alternative version of Islam as a religion of peace and not one committed to global jihad against the *kafir*. Instead, these moderates oppose only the limitless violence of the terrorist groups in practice, and not in the faulty, theological underpinning derived from the al-Hadees, a compilation of sayings attributed to the Prophet, but actually complied centuries afterwards.

The fourth sets of issues deals with the contextual situation that each country faces, for which it has to evolve its own responses. This does not mean regional or extra-regional cooperation is not required; in fact, the opposite is the case. But countries, at the end of the day, are selfish creatures; they do not fight each others' battles normally. Especially, not one where their past, and recent, conduct has been less than blemish-free. And, where they may be required to make a deal in order to get out of a 'bad' situation. Each country or a group of countries similarly placed must get their act together since the World (read the Western World) has limited attention and different priorities, thus expecting actual support may be unrealistic. Much as the killing of the 12 staff members of the *Charlie Hebdo* was horrific and was universally condemned, as it deserved, the killing of 2000 innocent civilians by the Boko Haram at the same time did not make any headlines or to even the main pages of the mainstream media. The many atrocities committed by the Pakistan-based and supported terrorists in India also generally fail to get a mention in discussions about terrorism, e.g., of the three large attacks in Mumbai, the 1993 blasts that killed 257, the largest carnage committed by terrorists till 9/11, and the 2006 Mumbai train blasts that killed 206—are off all radars. Even in the 2008 case, the focus was overwhelmingly on foreign victims. Nigeria, Chad, etc. are much worse off, with terrible attacks simply ignored, though their human costs are often staggering. The short point is that while naming and shaming must intensify, pre-empting attacks and the defeating of the terrorist groups would have to be done by the victims themselves.

We are sure that the readers would find the different articles thought-provoking, combining as it were, the perspectives of the policymakers, academics, real-time practitioners and leaders of governments. We hope that the coverage of the different aspects would bring out the multifaceted nature of terrorism globally, and locally. There is much to learn from different situations and approaches; ultimately, it has to be a combination of the universal and the national that would create conditions that would make the use of terror by disaffected groups, and the use of terrorist groups as instruments of proxy war by states, impossible to sustain.

PART I

THE WORLD VIEW

1

Terrorism: A Global Challenge

Shri Pranab Mukherjee
President of India

I am delighted to be amidst you this evening at the inauguration of the 2nd edition of the Counter-Terrorism Conference organised by the India Foundation in collaboration with Government of Rajasthan. It is heartening to note that this conference has brought together field operatives, senior officials from security agencies, policy makers, scholars and government leaders involved in counter-terrorism operations, planning and sensitisation to discuss ways of tackling global terror outfits.

Peace is the primary objective of rational consciousness as well as a moral universe. It is the foundation of civilisation and a necessity for economic success. And yet, we have never been able to answer a simple question: why does peace remain so elusive? Why has peace been so much more difficult to attain than conflict? These are the questions we need to ponder upon, both as a civilisation and as a society.

As the twentieth century closed down with a remarkable revolution in science and technology, we had some reason for optimism in the direction of peace and prosperity. That optimism has faded in the first fifteen years of this century. There is unprecedented turbulence across vast regions, with alarming increase in regional instabilities. The scourge of terrorism has reshaped war into its most barbaric manifestation. No corner in the world is now safe from this savage monster.

Terrorism is inspired by insane objectives, motivated by bottomless depths of hatred, instigated by puppeteers who have invested heavily in havoc through the mass murder of innocents. This is war beyond any doctrine, a cancer which must be operated out with a firm scalpel. There is no good or bad terrorism; it is pure evil.

Terrorism is undoubtedly the single gravest threat that humanity is facing today. Whether in Paris or Pathankot, terrorist attacks on democracies are attacks against fundamental values of liberty, freedom and universal brotherhood. Terrorism is a global threat which poses an unprecedented challenge to all nations. No cause can justify terrorist acts. It is imperative that the world acts in unison against terrorism, without political considerations. Therefore, there is a need to take a resolve to not justify terrorist means whatever be the reason or the source.

Till the end of the 20th century, terrorism had regional or national connotations. With the emergence of first al-Qaeda and now Islamic State (IS), those boundaries have shattered. Non-state actors are trying to be the state themselves, spreading radical ideologies across societies, using technologies to the fullest extent to attract youth. In such a scenario mere political and military strategies will not suffice. We need to take social, economic, religious and psychological aspects into consideration.

In the history of terrorism, the terrorist attack on the United States on September 11, 2001, is certainly a watershed moment. That moment defines the genesis of modern-day counter terrorism in the international context. From that single incident have flowed most of the interventions in the counter-terrorism sphere that we see happening at the international level as also at the regional and domestic levels. Faced with the spectre of terrorism, the Western world has undertaken a lot in terms of strategy and tactics and has achieved results also. We need to carefully examine and learn lessons from the success and failure of these strategies.

We may, at the same time, do well to remember that South Asia has been facing terrorist violence since decades in various forms. There is a peculiar nature to this terrorism. To counter that, South Asian countries, including India, have developed certain capabilities. We need to similarly discuss and deliberate on the effectiveness of these strategies and how these have impacted on our counter-terrorism capabilities.

An important aspect of counter-terrorism strategy is capacity building to prevent attacks through intelligence collection and collation, development of technological capabilities, raising of Special Forces and enactment of special laws. Though we have evolved certain mechanisms in this direction, there is scope for further intensifying these efforts.

Counter-terrorism is generally considered to be about tactics, weapons, force levels and intelligence gathering. While these things are important the predominant focus has to be on the political management of terrorism. This includes addressing issues of ideology and dealing with countries that sponsor or support terrorism. It is imperative that the world in one voice rejects all manifestations of terrorism, without distinction, and proscribes states that support or sponsor terrorism as an instrument of state policy.

We cannot also forget the fact that civil society is both the frontier and the battleground which has to be protected and saved. Fragmentation of civil society, rather than its consolidation, is not a wise strategy. The former course leads to radicalisation, which thereafter leads to competitive violence. Think tanks and civil society organisations have a larger role to play in this process of social integration. A pluralistic and inclusive society like India has long presented a model for multi-cultural living. It is for this reason that global terror outfits have not been able to find traction in India. We have, as a nation, to strengthen that plurality so that it acts as a bulwark against radical ideologies and thought processes.

These aspects highlight the fact that there is a need for comprehensive strategies and greater international cooperation to ward off future threats. Our counter-terrorism effort has to be more pointed, more focused, more objective and more professional. While doing so, there will always be a dilemma of whether we are threatening individual liberties or human rights. We have, therefore, to be judicious in protecting larger freedoms and democratic values. We need to fight this scourge at all levels—through shaping of public opinion, society building and evolving a concerted and integrated counter-terrorism policy premised on international cooperation in intelligence sharing. Needless to say, it also entails taking concerted action to shut down the financial networks that support and sustain terrorism.

I am confident that this conference shall deliberate on the challenges posed by global terror outfits, and examine the possibility of sharing capabilities with a view to combating larger dimensions of this threat. With these few words, I conclude. I wish you and the deliberations of the Conference all success. Jai Hind.

2

The Experience of Afghanistan

Abdullah Abdullah
Chief Executive of the Islamic Republic of Afghanistan

Across the world, political leaders, academic scholars and security experts are continuously engaged in debating, exploring and identifying effective policy options for combating and eliminating the growing threat of terrorism. I would like to focus on a discussion of the experiences of Afghanistan, in the global and regional contexts, to demonstrate how terrorism and its different manifestations have been instrumental in destabilising our otherwise peaceful country. By way of background, I would like to contextualise the complex threat of terrorism in Afghanistan against the backdrop of three periods: the Cold War; the post-Cold War; and the post-9/11.

The failures to follow through the missed opportunities for regional cooperation and the continued pursuit of zero-sum policies, characterise these three eras. Together, they have contributed to creating an enabling environment for terrorism and its utilisation as an instrument of state policy. Before the imposed conflicts, Afghanistan used to be one of the most peaceful countries in the region, despite our rife poverty. But we became one of the last victims of the Cold War, as the former Soviet Union invaded and occupied our country. In defence of our sovereignty and freedom, the Afghan people rose in resistance against the Soviets. And in our just war of liberation, we relied on those in the international community that shared our values and offered us resistance support.

The end of Cold War led to a power vacuum not only in our region but across the world. In such a situation, regional players began to act irresponsibly in an effort to protect their self-interest and to strengthen their strategic position in their respective regions. In effect, the end of the Cold War ushered in the beginning of regional cold wars, as opposed to a level playing field for regional cooperation. Ever since, states have often utilised proxy wars to serve their narrowly defined national security interests, disregarding "win-win" cooperation promoted by numerous UN Security Council resolutions backed by annual General Assembly debates. This situation has yet to change, even though lip-service is often given in support of a paradigm shift to results-oriented regional cooperation. Considering this dynamic, we are effectively facing a regional cold war where terrorism has become the principal instrument of projecting influence by some states against others. As a consequence, there is no universal appreciation of the grave danger, which terrorism poses to regional stability and international peace and security.

Although nations generally agree that terrorism threatens the security of the whole humanity, each state is developing its own homegrown capabilities to tackle the direct threat it faces within its milieu. They have been reluctant to adopt and implement a global counter-terrorism action plan, even though terrorism sees no borders, nationalities, religions, creeds or cultures. Ironically, however, in some cases, terrorism has helped bring old adversaries closer. And it has at times turned foes into allies and, in some cases, allies into foes. Such half-hearted measures have only addressed the symptoms rather than the causes of terrorism. That is why to be effective, I propose that each region assess the set of threats terrorism poses to their security and development and then agree to draft and implement a joint counter-terrorism action plan.

We know that there isn't much difference in the officially stated regional definition of what constitutes terrorism and how to counter it. Looking at how India, China, Pakistan, Iran, and others have defined terrorism, one can see that there isn't much difference in their individual definitions of the threat. Each of our neighbours has an elaborate counter-terrorism national action plan backed by strong counter-terrorism legislation. And at the regional level, terrorism has been often acknowledged to be a common enemy of all of us. We can conclude from the above that:

- The states in the region have appropriate counter-terrorism policies and laws.
- They operate at home, based on a common definition of terrorism.
- They have multilaterally reached a consensus on the nature of the threat and the need to counter it.

If that be so, then what bars us from collectively acting against terrorism, as we have witnessed the tragic terrorist attacks claiming many innocent lives in Kabul, Mumbai, Peshawar, Paris, Ankara, San Bernardino (California), and so many other places? In simple terms, why can't we regionalise our national counter-terrorism action plans?

Fortunately, we don't lack regional mechanisms of cooperation. The Heart of Asia Process, the Shanghai Cooperation Organisation (SCO), and the South Asian Association for Regional Cooperation (SAARC) are the appropriate mechanisms, through which we could organise our collective efforts in the fight against terrorism, drug trafficking, and other such threats. But we should operationalise these mechanisms, which Afghanistan has often demanded and stands ready to play its part in full measure in utilising them for effective regional counter-terrorism cooperation.

A few months before the tragedy of 9/11, I accompanied the national hero of Afghanistan, the late Commander Ahmad Shah Massoud, on a visit to Europe in April 2001. In our meetings with the senior leadership of the European countries, we warned that the premature international disengagement from Afghanistan had allowed state and non-state actors, including the Taliban and al-Qaeda, to turn our country into a no man's land where such groups daily terrorised our people, while using our soil as a launching pad for their global terrorist activities. Unfortunately, our warning to the West on the consequences of neglecting Afghanistan, failed to draw the support Afghanistan needed to free our land from the reign of terrorists and extremists. Consequently, the spillover effects of state failure in Afghanistan were far-reaching in the region and beyond. Its culmination came on September 11, 2001, when al-Qaeda, with a secure operational base in Afghanistan, attacked the United States homeland. And this was the exact scenario, which the late Commander Ahmad Shah Massoud had predicted and warned against.

As our brave forces continue fighting terrorism, we have relaunched a peace process. Our peace efforts are aimed at meeting the desire of every Afghan for freeing our country from an endless cycle of war and violence and to prevent the use of our soil as a platform for regional and global terrorist activities. On peace with the Taliban groups, our position is clear: Those Taliban groups, who are willing to join the process, they are welcome. While those, who refuse to do so, would be dealt with militarily. In effect, we do not differentiate between the Taliban and ISIS affiliated groups, and are firmly committed to fight and defeat any militant groups that share the ideology of al-Qaeda and ISIS.

As we continue our peace efforts, we invite all our neighbours to cooperate with Afghanistan. The National Unity Government of Afghanistan has repeatedly called on all stakeholders, including our neighbours, to commit the collective will and resources to confront what is a common security threat. Afghanistan has done more than lion's share. Last year, our courageous army and police forces sustained more than 7,000 casualties to fight the battles of the whole region against terrorism. Today, I renew our earlier calls on our neighbours to discontinue differentiating between "good terrorists" and "bad terrorists." We must put aside all double-standards in the fight against terrorism and apply our domestic counter-terrorism policies and laws to tackling the threat of terrorism at the regional and global levels.

I would like to pay tribute to the victims of all terrorist attacks across the world and to honour the sacrifices of our security forces, who have made the ultimate sacrifice in securing Afghanistan against terrorism over the past 14 years. Their precious losses have not gone in vain. I want the families and loved ones of the 'Fallen', including Afghans and our partners, to know that their irreplaceable losses have positively impacted on the life of every Afghan, including our women and children. We Afghans have done our part, as we have embraced democracy and daily fight to protect our democratic gains of the past 14 years. We are grateful for the support of our international partners and value the sacrifices of their soldiers for stability in Afghanistan and security of the world.

But our job is not yet done, as institutionalisation of peace, pluralism, and prosperity is a work in progress. Our success in this journey, which we share with our neighbours and international partners alike, will ensure the security of everyone. The Government and people of Afghanistan take immense pride in our ancient civilisational ties with the India, a country that is both our time-test friend and a strategic partner. We are grateful to the Indian Government for the recent provision of four helicopters, as well as for the completion of major infrastructure projects: the building of Afghanistan's Parliament, the Salma Dam in Herat, and two electricity sub-stations. In the months ahead, we look forward to India's new development aid to implement some of our signature economic infrastructure projects. This would further consolidate what has been achieved, while bolstering regional connectivity for increased transit trade and investment. Overall, Indian aid will go a long way in addressing Afghanistan's intertwined security and development needs, while enabling us to cooperate with the rest of the region in the fight against terrorism.

3

A Crime Against Humanity

Rajnath Singh
Home Minister, India

Today, much of the world is grappling with the scourge of terrorism and its dangerous consequences. Terrorism is seeking to destabilise the geo-political order in several parts of the world. It is doing so in pursuit of an insane interpretation of faith and philosophy that is violently anarchic and allergic to diversity which is the essence of humanity and its habitat.

I firmly believe that terrorism is a byproduct of a perverse mind. This perversion has no love for human beings or of humanity. Terrorism has no religion because religions do not allow crimes against humanity. Simply put, terrorism is a crime against humanity.

Unfortunately, while the world acknowledges the threat of terrorism, there is no consensus even on the definition of terrorism. The UN has adopted numerous resolutions to fight terrorism. All these resolutions amply show the resolve of the world. Sanctions stipulated by UN Security Council resolutions are often rendered ineffective by vested interests of some countries in the absence of a consensus definition of terrorism.

The challenge of terrorism gets compounded when certain states use it as an instrument of their foreign policy. They make perverse distinction between 'good' and 'bad' terrorists. When the states begin covertly raising and indoctrinating bands of youth and equipping them with lethal weapons and weapon systems of mass destruction to promote their geo-political agenda, the magnitude of threat amplifies many times. It makes the task of defeating terrorism much more difficult.

So long as some countries continue using terrorists as instruments to promote their geo-political agenda, the fight against terrorism would lack due resolve. The world must accept the reality without any loss of time that there is no 'good' terrorist. As we struggle to arrive at a consensus on relatively simpler issues such as the definition of terrorism, terror groups are becoming deadlier by the day. From traditional forms of terrorism, we are now witnessing cyberterrorism, narcoterrorism and bioterrorism. Use of dirty bombs also cannot be ruled out. Modern weapons, technology, and communications are being used by terror groups to enhance their lethality and impact.

Revolution in technology including the information technology has brought marked improvement in quality of life of the people. Ironically it has also given unprecedented destructive power in the hands of the terrorists. Now, they also operate in small nodes, widely dispersed, invisible and connected through digital networks. Never before in the human history, small groups of non-state actors could have access to so much destructive power.

We are a country full of diversity with multi-lingual, multi-religious and multi-ethnic society. These conditions are actively utilised by anti-national elements and other enemies to foment trouble in our country. To counter such threats we need to undertake sound preventive and responsive security measures. Most of the terrorist attacks in India emanate from Pakistan and it will have to show some sincerity and take concrete steps to rein in the various terror groups operating against India from its soil. If Pakistan takes concrete action against terrorists on its territory, it will not only improve the bilateral ties between both the countries but also bring peace and stability in the South Asian region. The government of India will stand by Pakistan if it takes decisive action against terrorists and their organisations.

For India, Mumbai and Pathankot terror attacks have signified a tectonic shift. Mumbai terror attack in 2008 brought terror across the seas to our economic capital causing large number of casualties on innocent civilian population. Likewise in the recent attack on Pathankot air base, there was a conscious effort to target sensitive assets of the country and also cause large scale casualties, thus taking the dynamics of terror attack in India a notch higher. However, it goes to the credit of our security forces and intelligence agencies that they not only prevented any damage to our capabilities and assets but also achieved it with minimum casualties to own security personnel. Security Forces also ensured that there were no casualties to families including trainees from friendly foreign countries. For such a brave act they deserve the highest accolades.

I can say this with conviction as terror attacks in the past on air bases of other countries such as Pakistan and Sri Lanka had led to major damages to their air assets including large number of casualties. After the Pathankot terror attack, the government is reviewing its counter-terror strategy. We are now formulating an effective strategy which would help in preventing our country from such terror attacks in future. We are fully equipped and prepared to deal with cross-border terrorism or any kind of terrorism. We are working on a national security strategy aiming to achieve seamless coordination between all the agencies.

We had advance intelligence input on Pathankot. It helped our security agencies in neutralising the possible impact of this terror attack. Proper assimilation, analysis and timely sharing of intelligence inputs hold key to any successful strategy against terrorism. The government is increasing its capabilities in this area as well. We are also stepping up vigil at our international borders and strengthening our border infrastructure to ensure fool proof security in the border areas.

Terrorism is hydra-headed monster fed by a massive supply of funds through different routes. We need to put a plug on the flow of funds to curb terrorism. Drug trafficking, hawala transactions and supply of counterfeit currency are some of the known sources of terror funding. It is a big challenge to cut the supply lines of terrorist organisations and their activities. There has to be global strategy and better coordination among like-minded nations against terrorism, if we want to disrupt the supply of funds to terror activities.

Given the ever increasing threat of terrorism in India, our national security strategy is now aiming at creating an environment which provides full opportunity for unhindered growth and development to every section of the society. We are also looking forward to create appropriate legal and structural frameworks to fight against the menace of terrorism. We want to ensure that all terror related cases are thoroughly investigated and followed up properly and regularly in the courts. Our guiding principle while handling terror related cases should be *"Koi Begunaah Fanse Nahi, Aur Koi Gunahgaar Bache Nahi"* (No innocent peson should be charged, no guilty person should be spared). We also solicit and appeal for full cooperation on issues pertaining to national security from the opposition too, because we need to rise above partisan politics on issues of national importance. Lack of consensus on matters like national security would adversely affect the country's national interest.

It is a cause of grave concern that the cyber world is being exploited by terror groups such as Daesh or ISIS to radicalise the gullible youth of our country. Since many security experts and intellectuals are present here, I appeal to all of you to use the word Daesh to mention ISIS in future because this terror organisation is seeking legitimacy through the word 'Islamic State'. The cyber world is also enabling 'lone wolf attacks' across the world. Exploiting the power of internet and ideological motivation, terror groups like Daesh and al-Qaeda have already flooded the internet with literature pertaining to bomb making and suicide attacks which present a risk of emergence of 'DIY' (do it yourself) terrorists. India also needs to be mindful of this possibility.

We have adopted a multi pronged strategy against the attempts to radicalise the youth of the country. On the one hand we have successfully de-radicalised our youth and on the other hand our security agencies have also taken action certain individuals for their links and association with terror organisations. The security experts believe that India's strategy against radicalisation is far more positive and effective than other countries of the world.

We are hopeful and firmly convinced that together we can neutralise any threat to our country. We also would like to assure various dignitaries and participants from friendly foreign countries that India stands firmly behind the international community in the fight against terrorism.

4

The Indian Perspective

S Jaishankar
Foreign Secretary, India

Deliberations on the challenges of counter-terrorism address different aspects of this issue, such as the role of technology and social media, financing and infrastructure, networking and cooperation, history and religion, as well as a range of national, regional and global responses. This paper focuses on how Indian diplomacy perceives this complicated problem, how we propose conceptually to address it, and what could be the possible policy options and challenges that may arise in that process. It is possible that some people may consider aspects of this approach overly ambitious. However, good diplomacy rarely sets itself a low bar, particularly on matters of vital national and international security.

Let me begin with the challenge itself. Terrorism is today widely seen as a truly global scourge. That in itself is a great improvement over an era where it was perceived in compartmentalised and geopolitical terms, as a law and order issue, an instrument of statecraft or an expression of beliefs. That era created the adage that one man's terrorist is another man's freedom fighter. No longer. The world does not accept today that any 'root cause' justifies terrorism. And it is becoming harder by the day to be openly selective on targeting terrorists. There are numerous reasons for these changes. Among them are experiences that have brought out an inability to 'manage' terrorism as a controlled exercise over any length of time. This bears some resemblance to how the world's approach to piracy evolved. Indeed, if we were to delve into a world of parallels, you may also recall how the challenge of chemical weapons or even that of treatment of prisoners unfolded in the global discourse. In these cases, nation states came to the conclusion that the benefits of exercising such options were outweighed by the costs of doing so. Equally, there was the realisation that the perpetrator could also end up as a victim. It is only when there is a broad sense of danger that the possibility of a regime to address that emerges.

We are, I believe, in that phase of deliberation today where the aim could be a consensus among the states of the international community to outlaw terrorism and delegitimise it as a tool of politics. Of course, such a line of thinking should not detract from specific and practical ways of countering terrorism. On the contrary, we should appreciate that this is a vital but currently missing piece of the puzzle. The counter-terrorism watch that many governments now keep will work best if it can be put in a larger construct. So far, however, the practical day-to-day aspect has dominated global response. But a framework will certainly help local action fit global norms, generating coherence in national responses and fostering international cooperation.

It is worth reflecting in this context that the world now has international conventions prohibiting the possession and use of chemical weapons and restricting those of nuclear weapons. At some point of time, both were regarded as utopian objectives. But now they have come to be accepted as an underpinning part of the contemporary international system. There are a number of other regimes which have emerged in recent years, including on narcotics trade, illegal financing, counterfeiting or infringing copyrights. So, the question we need to ask ourselves is why the challenge of countering terror cannot be broadly addressed.

The embryo of building such response exists in frameworks like the Financial Action Task Force (FATF) that sets standards with respect to combating money laundering and terrorist financing. Or the Egmont Group, which is an informal network of Financial Intelligence Units (FIU). Others such as the Al-Qaeda, Taliban and ISIS Sanctions Committee of the UNSC are also relevant instruments. But they do not yet provide an effective answer, most importantly, as they do not reflect a unified global response for reasons of national expediency.

The first serious attempt to approach terrorism from a regime perspective is our own initiative of tabling a Comprehensive Convention on International Terrorism at the United Nations. This was done two decades ago. Interestingly, the initiative has now gathered greater traction as the spectre of global terrorism appears more threatening. For those of you who may be unfamiliar with the CCIT, let me highlight its key elements. These are:

- It proposes to list several acts of unlawful and intentional violence that constitute an offence which all Parties are required to establish as criminal offences under their domestic laws.
- All Parties have to ensure these criminal acts are under no circumstances justifiable by considerations of a political, philosophical, ideological, racial, ethnic, religious or other similar nature. They are also to prohibit the establishment and operation of installations and training camps for the commission of such offences.
- The State Party, in the territory of which the alleged offender is present, has to submit the case without undue delay to its competent authorities for prosecution.
- Offences set forth in this Convention shall be deemed to be extraditable offences in any extradition treaty existing between any of the State Parties.

Any regime, to be effective, must enforce two key concepts: assigning responsibility and ensuring accountability. Obviously, that would require a set of norms that are universally applied and enforced. Now, the very basis of the contemporary international order is that nation states are its basic unit and each government takes responsibility for developments and actions within its territory. Indeed, when confronted with situations where that ability no longer exists, we term those polities as failed states and treat them as such. Furthermore, if actions emanating from a national territory impinge negatively on others, the government of that nation is, at the very least, pressed to probe and explain as the first step in a process of accountability. This holds true for nuclear and missile proliferation, for chemical weapons, for pandemics, and nowadays, even for suspect financial transactions. Why should that not be for countering terrorism?

This is now where the 'non-state' actor comes in; occasionally, as a genuine outcome of governance incapability, but more often as an escape clause. It isn't difficult in this modern age to trace the roots of a terrorist attack to a particular geography. The standing of those involved in terrorism in any society is not difficult to establish either. Clearly, it means something if they operate openly out of a big city with a known address, than if they live in a remote cave or an isolated jungle hideout. A paradigm, however, is not just about its human element. Terrorists use weapons that have clear sources of origin. They need financing and money usually leaves a trail. They deal with commodities; traders and brokers cannot be secrets. We have seen, in other areas, the effectiveness of controlling both upstream and downstream activities. Why not in countering terrorism?

In most cases, it is difficult for non-state actors to operate without the support and connivance of states. If we can move in the direction of a state-centred regime based on strict responsibility and accountability, that would certainly have a major impact on the freedom of non-state actors to propagate, operate and perpetrate. If nothing else, it would narrow the problem considerably and allow genuine non-state actors to be tackled in a more targeted manner.

That broad sense of responsibility is unfortunately still not there yet, even among nations that are themselves victims of terrorism. We have seen in the 1267 Committee and sometimes even in the FATF how specious arguments are advanced to block action on ostensibly technical grounds. But as the footprint of terrorism expands and assumptions of immunity erode, this is going to be harder to sustain. Remember, the non-state actor used to be a convenient excuse once upon a time in nuclear proliferation as well. As the dangers of that fig leaf became increasingly apparent, it was quietly abandoned. Since

9/11, a series of initiatives have pushed governments to assume their national responsibility, to seek help, share information and to cooperate with other governments to deny non-state actors access to nuclear material and facilities. A patchwork architecture of legal instruments has underpinned this shift. My argument is that many endeavours are deemed unrealistic—until they actually happen.

Even as we work to advance the prospects of a CCIT, there are a number of interim steps that can be taken. The most important of them is to exercise the ability to cause reputational damage. Naming and shaming must be carried out relentlessly in the case of perpetrators, supporters and connivers of terrorism. Tolerance for double standards on this issue must be equally frankly exposed. After all, this works in other areas—whether we speak of financial defaulters, nuclear proliferators, illegal traders or just regular violators of law. The pressure of international public sentiments can make the costs of terrorism escalate well beyond the calculations of its practitioners. A second and related activity is to use diplomacy to isolate those indulging in terrorism. Eliciting statements of solidarity when attacks happen and expressions of policy independent of happenings have a value often underestimated. To do this effectively, it is important that we do not ascribe characteristics to terrorism—whether they be of religion, region or ethnicity.

What may work in the case of states will obviously not always do so with non-state forces. They have no reputation to lose. If anything, they thrive on a bad one. Clearly, a different menu of diplomatic options has to be considered in their case. The key point here is that terrorists, like all other creatures, need an ecosystem to grow in. Admittedly, there are broader debates of countering extremism and radicalisation that are vital to the preventive aspects of terrorism. But more often than not, it is the state that provides the oxygen for non-state activities. Moving beyond discouraging state sponsorship of terrorism, the next step is therefore to build effective inter-state cooperative mechanisms to combat it. That is already work in progress, admittedly in its early stages. But there are issues today before the international community that beg answers. Where do potential terrorists go for training? Or how does their financing work?

In many cases, we know the answers and yet choose to look away. Of equal concern is that our reaction to terrorism in some geographies is different from others. Old habits may die hard but new realities cannot be wished away. We are currently witnessing the impact of the Middle East on Europe, a development waiting to happen and yet not anticipated! Another caution worth reflecting on is to resist the temptation of buying peace at home by striking deals elsewhere. Terrorism should not be confused for social media, with our responses limited to the "trending" activities. Because new threats have emerged does not mean that the tested ones have gone away. At the end of the day, much would depend on persuading states to refrain from using terrorism as a card in the games that nations play. For those who continue to be tempted, all I can say is that is enough history to demonstrate that the care-givers of terrorism are bitten by those they nurture.

Countering terrorism is a priority imperative for Indian diplomacy. The role of diplomacy in facilitating intelligence cooperation and building national capabilities cannot be overstated. We have made major strides in putting in place practical cooperation with a number of countries. This is a sensitive and cumulative exercise, of building trust and habits of working together. Our counter-terrorism and security dialogues which bring together experts from all the relevant fields in regular bilateral and multilateral interactions are an important diplomatic tool. So too is the daily work of forums such as the FATF and UN Committees to deny terrorists financing and other forms of support. And my key point today: do not ignore the utility of lawfare—the power of legal arguments—in the menu of counter-terrorist solutions, or the impact of world opinions.

The 9/11 Commission brought out two major limitations in government's response to terrorism that I take to be universal observations: those of imagination and those of integration. The first is an infinite proposition. But on the second, we in India, are moving to a more 'whole of the government' approach towards countering terrorism. I can say from personal experience that this is reflected in the manner in which we have approached developments earlier in the year. That we have a special envoy dedicated to this range of issues also speaks for itself. The problem that the world faces is that while the bad guys think global, the good guys still think national, sometimes still departmental. Encouraging a 'whole of the world' approach in countering terrorism is one of the major goals of Indian diplomacy. We have, admittedly, a long journey ahead but every journey begins with the first steps.

5

The Malaysian Viewpoint

Datuk Nur Jazlan Mohamed
Deputy Minister of Home Affairs, Malaysia

In January 2016, the Singapore government unveiled that it had uncovered a terror cell operating in the country, comprising of migrant Bangladeshi workers. This revelation did not just mark the first time that a foreign terror cell had been uncovered, but more significantly, that it was a major threat posed by foreign migrant workers plying their trade in the city state. As both our regional economic ties prosper, it never crossed our minds that we would be faced with such a situation. Like our southern neighbour, we in Malaysia are deeply concerned by this, as we have been a destination of choice for many south Asian migrant economic workers over the years.

We are now at a time when undoubtedly the threat of radicalism and terrorism is increasingly widespread and dangerously localised. Let us not be lulled into thinking that these are separate issues, for which they are, but only in definition. The destructive violence of terrorism, radicalisation of ideologies and the propagation of extremism, are all cancerous mutations of the ideas of a misguided few, whose actions have, as we have seen only too recently, caused pain, suffering and the loss of many innocent lives.

Extremism and indeed radicalism have also found their way into our communities, with the potential to destroy the very fabric of order and harmony, and leave in its place, only chaos and destruction. Now, more than before, special measures are required to halt the spread of terrorism and to preserve and maintain peace and stability.

The attacks in Paris on the night of Friday 13 November 2015, the bombings that took place on 12 January 2016 in Istanbul and the multiple explosions that shook Jakarta on 14 January 2016 are but recent examples that clearly show the brutal reality of terrorism and violent extremism, and that it may at times exist non sequitur. Let us be acutely aware that acts of terrorism are insidiously random, always violently ruthless and equally destructive. While Malaysia continues to enjoy peace and security, avoiding the grave consequences of terrorism domestically, we acknowledge that it is the result of the combined and concerted effort of various law enforcement and intelligence agencies. Nevertheless, even as we continue to remain vigilant, monitoring and securing the safety of our nation domestically, we are committed and will continue to participate actively in initiatives against terrorism globally.

Malaysia's stand point against radicalism and extremism is clear and remains unchanged. The emergence of an entirely new breed of radicalism, groups and terrorists who flog religious commandments as their battle cry, carry with them a new kind of threat to both national and international security. In the most certain of terms, I state that Malaysia is strongly opposed to any form of terrorism, especially terrorist acts perpetrated in the name of Islam.

Malaysia stands resolute against the actions of terrorist groups that exploit Islam through the continuous abuse of Islamic edicts and precepts to justify its acts of violence. Indiscriminate attacks on innocent civilians and non-combatants are clearly acts of cowardice. It is with disdain and disgust that such acts are viewed, and Malaysia stands firm in completely and unequivocally rejecting any attempt to associate Islam with the violent extremism perpetrated by terrorists against innocent Muslims and non-Muslims alike. My government is prepared to cooperate with the international community in the war against terrorist and terrorism, whether domestic or abroad, and will act with full force against those who threaten the peace and stability of the country and the security of its people. While the use of force is somewhat a necessity at any given time, our policy in the war against terror is not merely confined to battles on the ground but also includes, in large part, active engagement in de-radicalisation programmes and to counter extremist ideas and ideologies.

There is thus a dire need for more potency in addressing the growing concern of terrorism, in all its guises and forms. A solution that deals not only with the devastative after effects of radicalism and extremism but a solution that reaches deep into the labyrinth of ideological confusion, a confusion that, in the first place, gave life to radicalism. We need a solution that is able to cut a clearer path to a more peaceful and moderate resolution.

Malaysia has the proud record of eradicating the communist guerrilla threat as well as successfully overcoming other numerous incidences of extremism, religious and otherwise, in the many years following its independence. Strategies which we have employed, while largely offensive tactically, have always included outreach-type programmes to counter extremist ideologies at its source. By this, I mean programmes to reach into the psyche of extremists. We may know "how" an extremist might act in a given scenario but we may not necessarily know "why". The "why" brings us into a battle of minds, of emotions and of personal leanings.

My government has taken significant steps to improve the effectiveness of its counter-terrorism measures. In 2012, we enacted the Security Offences (special measures) Act, 2012 to replace the Internal Security Act, 1960. The objective of this legislation is to ensure matters of national security are addressed effectively, including terrorism, while adhering to international standards.

Another important legislation is POTA—the Prevention of Terrorism Act, 2015. POTA is a newly introduced preventive law to specifically provide for the prevention of the commission or support of terrorist acts involving listed terrorist organisations in a foreign country or any part of a foreign country. We also introduced the Special Measures against Terrorism in Foreign Countries Act, 2015 or SMATA. The act provides for special measures to deal with persons who engage in the commission or support of terrorist acts involving listed terrorist organisations in a foreign country or any part of a foreign country. The special measures shall apply to any person who travels to Malaysia, or who travels or intends to travel to a foreign country from or through Malaysia.

While Malaysia has already had several existing laws that can be used to take action against terrorists, the contemporary nature of these of threats, in particular those posed by IS or Daesh, attests that we need new preventive solutions in addition to punitive action. In line with our efforts to counter present-day extremism in cyberspace, our honourable deputy prime minister recently announced Malaysia as a regional counter messaging centre or hub to develop and disseminate counter extremist messages. The centre shall begin its operations in May 2016.

Malaysia has long been recognised as a beacon of moderate Islam, particularly through the manifestation of how this peaceful religion is practiced within our society. Our prime minister, the honourable Dato' Sri Najib Tun Abdul Razak, during his speech at the 65th United Nations General Assembly in 2010, introduced the Global Movement of Moderates or GMM as a new approach in international relations and foreign policy, with the main goal of applying perspectives and frameworks of moderation to realise world peace and harmony. Malaysia recently hosted the International Conference on De-Radicalisation and Countering Violent Extremism in Kuala Lumpur on 25 and 26 January 2016. The conference successfully concluded that the global community must come together with collegiate urgency, to share expertise and intelligence and to forge a closer regional cooperation in order to fight the issue. On that note and during the conference, I had the pleasure to meet with colleagues representing various countries and among the key issues we deliberated, was to work closely together in curbing the menace that extremist groups such as Daesh brings to our country and society. Their success in radicalising young men and women, often from stable and educated families, not only threatens the safety of our citizens, but also tears apart what we are as a nation.

We must change the ideology of terrorists and extremists to make them realise that their interpretation of their cause or religious precepts are a deviation from the truth. As a point in discussion, the interpretation of jihad. A dangerous chasm in proper religious guidance has allowed radicals and violent extremists to corrupt and exploit a minority of believers into deviationist and violent acts of terrorism in the name of jihad. It is this that we must approach, not only with the punitive rod of enforcement but also with the power of enlightenment.

In recognising this and the need for effective de-radicalisation and rehabilitation programmes, Malaysia, using a multi-faceted approach, designed a special module under a programme for the rehabilitation of terrorists. The de-radicalisation approach is underlined under the UN Security Council Resolution 2178 that requires UN member countries to formulate a program for returning foreign terrorist fighters.

In the rightful pursuit of a safer world for everyone, we see nations, pursuing with unrelenting vigour, terrorists and terror groups, hunting down radicals and extremist alike, putting military and law enforcement in the forefront of the battle against radicalism, extremism and the violent clash of ideologies. We must stand united in combating terrorism and violent extremism. Too many innocent lives have been sacrificed at the altar of misconceived ideologies. These attacks only reaffirm the urgent need for the international community to step up, to do more, to stand firm and united in the global war against terrorism.

Malaysia stands steadfast against terror, against radicalism and against extremism in whatever mould it finds and defines itself in. In countries where the war on terror continues to be fought, where misconceived ideologies and violent extremism are continually battled, Malaysia stands united. In Jakarta, Malaysia stands united. In Istanbul, Malaysia stands united. In Paris, Malaysia stands united. And in India, Malaysia stands united with the government and people of India. To other nations who continue to do battle against terrorism and extremism, I say, Malaysia stands united with you. We the people of Malaysia stand shoulder to shoulder with the people of India and the global community to actively de-radicalise.... Providing a massive dose of prevention to terrorism!

6

Fighting Terrorism: Adopt the Right Strategies

Ajit Doval
National Security Advisor, India

Terrorism is a very important issue that probably affects all of us from individuals to the civil societies, to the nations and humanity at large. On September 20, 2001, President Bush, while addressing the American Congress, said 'we are going to wage a war, a global war against terrorism'. In these 15 years, the world has tried to unite itself against the menace which every country felt was to be fought and to be defeated.

Where are we in these 15 years? An analysis of the incidents and casualties that occurred in 2015, indicates that a dramatic increase of about three hundred and twenty percent from the incidents and casualties that took place in 2001. A look at the geographical spread indicates that terrorism has now spread to areas where it never existed in the past. If you see the money that has been spent by the states, probably it has compounded manifold. It all leads us to a one very basic question: When the history of the world will be written 100 years hence, will it be said that these were the wasted 15 years in which we paid a very heavy cost in terms of thousands of people who died in this war against terrorism and which destabilised the societies and the regions which had been very stable in the past? This has created a sense of insecurity in the civil societies and probably, there is no end to this dark terror in the immediate future.

Are there any lessons that we can learn from our experience of the past few years? One idea that comes to mind is that in fighting terrorism, we must always do the right things. That is important. But what is more important is that we should avoid doing the wrong things. Is it that the state, which is one of the very important stakeholders in this war against terror did more things that were wrong than the things that were right? And is that the reason why the total end result of this entire struggle and effort and the cost that we have paid in lives and money has been negative? The question has no easy or straightforward answer.

But one thing, one illustration that comes to mind is that when the states feel that they can outsource the instrument of coercion to some of the non-state actors to achieve their strategic or political objectives, 15 years have proven that to be the most counter-productive strategy. Any country, anywhere in the world, which has tried this strategy, has found to its cost that it has boomeranged and hit back with vehemence.

Which are the countries, societies and places from where the terrorists get the ideological, material and financial support, as also sanctuaries to operate from? Certain terrorist groups also get support in international forums, making it difficult to initiate action in the global fora against those people whose guilt has been fully established. That is why the war against terrorism is a difficult one to win.

Policies and strategies are important. Also, the tactics are important. Strategy without the right tactics is the shortest way to commit suicide, just as tactics without strategy is the noise before defeat. We have made more noise than we have made the plan for success. If the countries of the world have to defeat the menace of terrorism, everything that sustains this phenomena has to be destroyed and smothered—be it the men, the human resource that is recruited, that is trained and brainwashed or be it the material, the explosives or the guns, or the political and ideological support that they receive. Unfortunately, the world has still not coped with these vital issues. We have gone to the peripheries, we have tried to find solutions treating the symptoms, but we have not done the essential analysis as to what is vital and what is desirable. Unless we firmly deal with the vitals that sustain the phenomenon of terrorism, we are not going to touch the desirables. And vital is the need for an international institutionalised mechanism to provide deterrence to those states that provide support to terrorism, in some form or the other.

In terms of security, terrorism impacts us all. Of equal import is to have suitable response mechanisms to counter terror. In terrorism, what is happening to us is the phenomenon that we are talking about. What we are actually not talking about is what our response should be. As of now, our response perhaps has not been what it should be. However, we now have the empirical data of the last 15 years to analyse and study. Through its analysis, we will perhaps have a clearer insight on where things went wrong and what could be done to set them right.

7

The Agony of Afghanistan

Amrullah Saleh
Former Head, National Directorate of Security, Afghanistan

"The wound is the place where the light enters you," is a saying from Rumi, the 13th Century Persian poet and Sufi mystic. As far as experiencing terror is concerned, we wake up with the pain of it every day. So the quote from Rumi is relevant, and you know that Rumi is the universal sign of Afghanistan whose message of love, harmony, co-existence, oneness of souls and destiny remains relevant today and will remain so forever.

Afghanistan is, unfortunately, the other aspect of this saying—it is the wound of the region and the wound needs healing. It has been the wound for a very long time now. That healing should come because we are a part of humanity. We have a stake in peace. We have given and we are giving massive sacrifices, but something is amiss. The wound remains and it is not healing. In this paper, I will focus on what is wrong, so that things may be set right.

In deliberations across the globe the flavour of the season is the ISIS, and the Taliban seems to have been relegated in the consciousness of the world. However, the Taliban cannot and must not be delisted from the terror index, despite the rise of the ISIS as there is little to distinguish between the two. If one leaves a bottle of Coke and another of Pepsi out in the open for a few hours, it is impossible thereafter to distinguish the one from the other. That is how different the Taliban and the ISIS are from each other.

Let us look at some of the striking similarities between the two. The ISIS destroyed pre-Islamic heritage in 2015; the Taliban destroyed the Bamiyan Buddha statues of Afghanistan in 2001. So both have a common hate against history. The ISIS massacred Yazidis and continues to massacre minorities; The Taliban massacred Shias when it took over Mazar-i-Sharif in the 1990s. Both groups exploit regional geo-politics to defend their ideological space and maintain cash flows and financing. It's as relevant to ISIS as it is to the Taliban. The ISIS occasionally burns a human being, to foster fear, whether it's a Jordanian pilot or a Turkish soldier. Similarly, the Taliban in the 1990s resorted to scorched earth policies displacing literally hundreds of thousands from their villages and burning entire villages in order to allow the al-Qaeda to create training camps in Afghanistan. I wonder why those memories seem so distant, when they occurred not so many years ago.

The ISIS created Khilafat; The Taliban created Emarat. Literally, there is no difference between the concept of a Khilafat and an Emarat, which means both groups are absolute, their concept of governance is the exclusion of everybody considered as 'other' in the society. Both groups are born out of state collapse. Both groups are born after the result of military intervention of a global power in a specific region at a specific time. Having said this, I wonder why there is no flavour to keep the Taliban on the terrorist list and why we just sometimes single out a few individuals in the Taliban or a part of them called as the Haqqani group. The entire lot of Taliban must be branded terrorists. The members of the Taliban are similar to the ISIS in their ideological leanings and in their conduct, whether it be beheadings, spectacular bombings, crime, extortion, etc. The methods are exactly the same.

Now let me focus on what has gone wrong at the international, regional and national levels, which needs to be set right. At the international level, the military intervention post-9/11, no doubt, brought enormous prosperity to Afghanistan, compared to the period of Taliban rule, but it did not defeat the Taliban. The post-9/11 intervention pushed the Taliban from Afghan territory into Pakistani territory. And in Pakistan, the job was sub-contracted to the Pakistani military, which in my view was a wrong partner to do the job. Rather than dismantling the network, the Pakistani military provided it with succour and support.

There were soft measures too, undertaken against terrorism. In the United Nations, Resolution 1373 asks member states to take specific measures against terrorism and not provide safe havens and finance to terrorist groups nor show sympathy nor allow any direct or indirect type of support for them. Despite that, Afghanistan's neighbour Pakistan openly permits the collection of donations for the Haqqani network and others in Afghanistan. When the Taliban negotiators travelled to Qatar, they used Pakistani passports. So the question is, "Why the world has not been very firm on implementation of Resolution 1373?" That is one of the areas in which the world has collectively failed.

At the regional level, immediately after 9/11, when the NATO and US military came to Afghanistan, the region was bypassed except for one country: Pakistan. For historical, logistical, locational and geo-strategic reasons, Pakistan was chosen as a partner of the war against terror. The al-Qaeda was identified as the priority number one and not the Taliban, because the US believed that it was the al-Qaeda and not the Taliban that had been directly involved in facilitating the attacks that occurred on 9/11. However, the Taliban was involved, as can be seen by the fact that the Taliban was given an offer to be a part of the power structure in Afghanistan, on the condition that this group renouncesits association with the al-Qaeda, but it refused to do so and preferred to fight, rather than break with the al-Qaeda. That by itself is a very firm and solid evidence, a circumstantial evidence at least, that the Taliban was involved in the 9/11 attacks and that the group had given its consent and approval for such type of attacks.

A counter argument to the above is given by people who state that the Taliban is a local group and is fighting only because it is under pressure. That belies an understanding of the Taliban. If allowed to come back, this group will do exactly what it did in the 1990s. This disconnect in the region is still hurting the global war on terror because, as it has been pointed out by innumerable analysts, selectivity in fighting terror has created a space for terror groups and it has also enabled them to boost their presence. So we have come up with puerile terminologies such as good terrorist, bad terrorist, pro-me-terror, pro-you-terror, et al., and that has basically taken all of us hostage.

So, what is the way forward? Again I would like to quote Rumi, who said, "where there is a ruin, there is a hope for a treasure." Afghanistan is seen as a ruin of the region, but the hope of the treasure remains and can be fulfilled. A solution to the problem in Afghanistan lies in engaging with the Government of Afghanistan and its people to bring stability and to create a mindset in the terror groups that they cannot win. A return of Taliban in any form will only boost the morale of terror groups and will lead to further violence and bloodshed.

Second, the buzzword these days about the situation of Afghanistan is reconciliation and peace process and settlement. The Afghans have stood with the world as far as the fight on terror is concerned. Before that, the Afghans stood with the West and with the rest of the world in the fight against communism. Our expectation from our allies today is that they should not be observers, facilitators, or bystanders when the process of reconciliation is being talked about. They should stay with Afghanistan as an ally and not treat Afghanistan as an egg basket, because the state collapse in Afghanistan goes back to the 1980s where the country fought for a cause and thought that a new state would be built with the assistance of our allies. So we are not purely an egg basket and a case of charity. We have played a major role and we are playing a major role for a global cause.

Thirdly, the involvement of non-state actors, specifically the Taliban will be counter productive. The talk of including the Taliban in bilateral dialogues with our neighbours or multilateral or regional dialogues will set a very bad precedence. The entire achievement of the post 9/11 intervention in Afghanistan could well be wiped out or considerably weakened, if the Taliban were to enter the corridors of power. Coopting a terrorist group in a power sharing arrangement, when that group, on a daily basis, is involving itself in acts of violence against children, women and civilians undermines the stability that Afghanistan has achieved, and creates a perception that it is another Afghan government-in-exile and negates the investment that the world has made in Afghanistan post-9/11.

The solution is not the empowerment of these violent non-state actors who thought nothing of destroying the electric grid in winter, depriving the people of warmth in the bitter cold. The solution is remaining committed to the Afghan state. Afghanistan is functioning and will continue to function. The Afghan security forces are giving the largest number of sacrifices for a cause which is still global and which is still hurting the entire human community. Calling the Taliban action as insurgency or rebranding it in any other form will not change the substance of this terrorist group.

Finally, I would like to leave a message for the policymakers in Pakistan. Our message to Islamabad has always been "work with Kabul. Bring an end to the recognition of the Taliban Emirate which is sitting in Qatar and which is sitting in Karachi". Whatever grievances Pakistan has, the solution will be a state-to-a-state dialogue. Whatever the magnitude of the problem will be, again the solution will be a state-to-a-state dialogue. The biggest challenge we have is not the superficial and shallow relationship that Islamabad has with Kabul, but the strategic alliance it has with the Taliban which has not ended. Afghanistan needs that alliance to end and it needs Islamabad and Kabul to talk as two governments and remove the non-state factor from the relationship. That will bring a type of a stability and an understanding in this region which will end terrorism and open enormous economic opportunities for all in the region.

8

The Bangladeshi Initiative to Combat Terrorism

Md. Shahriar Alam
State Minister, Ministry of Foreign Affairs, Bangladesh.

Bangladesh strongly believes that terrorism and extremism remain as major impediments to global peace and development. Terrorism, both in its magnitude and proliferation, is one of the gravest challenges not only to international peace and security but also to human security. Regionally also, we are facing the challenges of terrorism as evidenced by the terror attack on an air base in Pathankot in India and in a series of attacks in Afghanistan. While we express our deep condolences to the bereaved families, we should not limit ourselves here. The countries in the region with the help and support of the international community ought to further strengthen their efforts to make sure that no more precious lives, no more brothers and sisters of ours, die from such heinous incidents. While we remain vigilant against such unmindful acts of highest condemnation, let me emphasise that terrorism cannot and should not be linked or stigmatised to any religion, civilisation, nationality or ethnicity.

Today, thirty percent of the global population lives in South Asia. People of all religions peacefully coexist in this region. But over the past 100 years, we have witnessed from time-to-time religious, ideological and linguistic intolerance in this region. All countries in this region are thereby, somehow affected. However, India has suffered greatly, due to terrorist attacks from all directions. But it has faced terrorist intolerance with a great degree of patience and forbearance.

In Bangladesh too, our path to attaining peace has never been smooth. At times, we face fundamentalism and anti-state, anti-democracy commotions of anti-liberation forces. We have been victims of terrorist attacks. However, under the directives of Hon'ble Prime Minister Sheikh Hasina, we have resolutely confronted the challenges. As a result, we managed to unite the people of Bangladesh against these vicious incidents and have put in sustained efforts to overcome violence, restore law and order and uphold democracy. Our present Government's position on terrorism is clear-cut and categorical. Bangladesh condemns terrorism in all its forms and manifestations. The present Government of Bangladesh, under the able leadership of Prime Minister Sheikh Hasina, has been continuing and will continue to follow a zero-tolerance policy against terrorism and violent extremism. Bangladesh pursues a value-driven foreign policy that adheres to and promotes peace, democracy, secularism, freedom, human rights, good governance and social justice, a culture of peace and non-violence, inter-faith and inter-cultural dialogues as well as ethnic and religious tolerance to combat violent extremism and fundamentalism. Bangladesh also continues to advocate for relevant human rights and humanitarian principles in the counter-terrorism efforts. We would continue to champion innovative socio-economic interventions including attaining sustainable development goals (SDGs), micro-finance-based livelihood for women, women empowerment, education and job creation for all and a strong legal institutional regime to counter the root causes of extremism and terrorism.

Here, I would like to briefly enumerate the endeavours and measures taken so far by Bangladesh to combat terrorism. At the national level, Bangladesh has undertaken a series of legal, policy and administrative steps to combat terrorism including its financing. Over the past several years, Bangladesh has developed a robust legal regulatory and institutional regime to combat terrorism and violent extremism. The Anti-Terrorism Act, 2009, further amended in 2012 and 2013, provides a legal foundation for comprehensive counter-terrorism measures. The Government has also promulgated Anti-Terrorism Rules of 2013 to specify the responsibility of the respective agencies for implementation of the Act. The Anti-Terrorism Act of 2009 is further complemented by the Prevention of Money Laundering Act of 2012 and Mutual Legal Assistance Act of 2012. Alongside, the Government has promulgated Money Laundering Prevention Rules, 2013 and the Mutual Legal Assistance in Criminal Matters Rules, 2013. A list of predicate offences has been extended in the Money Laundering Prevention Act, 2012 which includes among others, terrorism and terrorist financing. Bangladesh is also keen in devising a comprehensive national counter-terrorism strategy paper. Our motto is to deny sanctuary to terrorists. Our Government is also currently implementing a national counter-radicalisation strategy through imparting education, women empowerment and propagation of secular and moderate cultural values creating a mindset of tolerance, friendliness and love in line with our culture of peace—a resolution which we table every year at the UNGA.

At the grass-root level, the Government of Bangladesh has engaged the religious scholars to de-motivate the terrorist sympathisers, having belief in their self-made cause. As a part of the policy, the Religious Affairs Ministry arranges religious gatherings to highlight the negative impact of militancy. In order to reform the Madrasa education system, the Bangladesh Government has revised and modernised the Madrasa curriculum along with the mainstream education focusing on employment opportunities. In addition, the Education Ministry is going to organise teacher-student conventions at district level and other local government units on creating awareness to prevent militancy and will incorporate essays and short stories against terrorism in the textbooks. The Information Ministry is making documents, short films, dramas, advertisements and video clips against militancy and putting those on the media to build up awareness against radical ideas. The Government is also working for building the capacity of the relevant law enforcement and prosecution agencies to effectively combat transnational organised crimes including circulation of illegal arms and fake currencies.

Let me now deliberate on our association with the international and regional counter-terrorism efforts. Given the transnational nature and spread of terrorism, no single country can adequately contain this scourge. It is therefore imperative to embark on both global and regional cooperation. Internationally, Bangladesh is a party to all 14 universal anti-terrorism instruments and has ratified the UN Convention against Transnational Organised Crimes as well. The Government of Bangladesh also supports the work of UN in the effective implementation of the Security Council Resolution 1267. We have banned all global terror outfits blacklisted by the 1267 Committee and we are keeping a close eye on any suspicious activity. Domestically, the Government of Bangladesh has banned several groups such as Harkat-ul-Jihad-al-Islami (HuJI) Bangladesh, Jagrata Muslim Janata Bangladesh, Jamaat-ul-Mujahideen Bangladesh, and Shahadat-e-al-Hikma. Many of the perpetrators of bombing incidents including their main leaders have been tried and the security forces continue to act against terrorists, on receipt of information with respect to their alleged hideouts.

Bangladesh has also been very active in the South Asian region in areas ranging from building the state's capacity to prevent and combat terrorism to strengthening the role of regional organisations in this regard. Under the aegis of SAARC, cooperation in the areas of security and counter-terrorism related issues has been institutionalised through a number of legal instruments including the SAARC Regional Convention and the Suspension of Terrorism, an additional protocol to this convention. A particular focus of these instruments is to combat organised transnational crimes including terrorism, human trafficking and illegal trafficking of drugs and narcotics. Bangladesh has also initiated regional counter-terrorism instruments under the BIMSTEC (Bay of Bengal Initiative for Multi-Sectoral Technical and Economic Cooperation) Counter-Terrorism Convention. Member states have signed the counter-terrorism convention titled BIMSTEC Convention on Cooperation in Combating International Terrorism, Transnational Organised Crime and Illicit Drug Trafficking. Bangladesh has so far organised two regional seminars in collaborating with the UN in promoting the UN counter-terrorism strategy during the last seven years.

In line with its principal position, Bangladesh condemns all terrorist acts including the killing of innocent civilians, particularly women and children, destruction of property, cultural and religious sites in parts of Iraq and Syria by the ISIL and other individual groups and entities. Bangladesh takes notes of the United Nations Security Council Resolution 2170 and its successor resolution 2178 adopted in 2014 at the Security Council Summit. In compliance with the United Nations Security Council Resolution 2170 and 2178, Bangladesh remains on guard against a possible enlistment of our nationals with the ISIS and other international terrorist organisations as foreign terrorist fighters (FTF). In this context, Bangladesh remains committed to implement through its UNHCR national mechanism, the relevant provisions of the Security Council Resolution 2178 on prevention on entry, transit, recruitment, organising, transporting and equipping of the FTF and the financing of their travel and activities.

Bangladesh also extends full support to any initiative under the UN umbrella to combat the FTF. Bangladesh will continue to work closely with the United Nations counter-terrorism bodies and its international partners including at the regional level towards a greater international cooperation for information sharing and capacity building in order to address the FTF threats to peace and security. Bangladesh has also complied with the United Nations Security Council Resolution 1373 which was a counter-terrorism measure against al-Qaeda, Taliban and other allied groups, following the aftermath of the 9/11 terrorist attacks.

Bangladesh and India have enjoyed excellent friendly relations for the last seven years or so. In fact, we are enjoying the best of relations. Our two countries have been cooperating in all sectors of political, security, economy and cultural relations. The historic visit of Prime Minister Shri Narendra Modi has taken the relationship to a new level. The security cooperation, particularly, has been a high point of the bilateral relations. As a part of that, we are working closely to expand our bilateral cooperation to fight terrorism as well. It featured prominently in the discussion between Prime Minister Sheikh Hasina and Prime Minister Shri Narendra Modi when the latter visited Dhaka in June 2015. In that joint declaration, the two

Prime Ministers expressed satisfaction at the unparalleled level of cooperation between the two countries on security-related issues, and reaffirmed their countries' unequivocal and uncompromising position against extremism and terrorism in all forms and manifestations as well as their commitment to cooperate with each other by sharing information about the groups and persons indulging in terrorism. This encapsulates the joint political commitment to combat terrorism. At various high-level meetings, the two sides agreed that terrorism posed a threat to both countries and that there was a need to cooperate closely to tackle this menace.

The growing number of dedicated joint institutional mechanisms between India and Bangladesh in various areas related to security is enabling us to take more coordinated, targeted action-oriented steps. The multi-tiered consultative mechanism and regular meeting between the heads of border guarding agencies are in place between our two countries and are working smoothly to take our security sector cooperation forward. We have built up a cooperative security framework by signing a good number of security-related agreements and MoUs which specially address the issues of terrorism. Among these, we have a dedicated agreement on combating international terrorism, organised crime and illicit drug trafficking under the aegis of which specific actions are being taken. The Bardhaman blast case in West Bengal was a good example of our close cooperation in this sector.

Terrorism and violent extremism are a result of critical and complex socio-political disorders and their solution is even more complicated. Counter-radicalisation work is vital in minimising the threat of extremism. The struggle is ultimately ideological. The terrorist groups and non-state actors continually evolve their modes of operation and devise more complex ways to carry out their heinous acts with deadlier consequences. The use of technology, information and social media as well as a nexus between terrorist networks, non-state actors and trans-national criminals pose newer challenges to the state operatives and the traditional approaches to terrorism. Therefore, the need for coordinated action by all the countries cannot be more important. The counter-terrorism agenda thus requires to be evolved through continued dialogue and must be strengthened through global and regional capacity development, coordinated approaches and sharing of best practices.

The Bangladesh Government's effort to combat extremist activities of the radical groups is high on the agenda. All our efforts are being made to besiege the activities and expansion of extremism inside Bangladesh and its expansion beyond the border. We are optimistic that regional cooperation including cooperation at all bilateral levels, especially among the neighbouring countries, would help reduce and contain the terrorism, if not wipe it out completely. Bangladesh remains committed to this cause.

9

The View from Iran: The Need for a Collaborative Approach

Ibrahim Rahimpour
Deputy Minister for Asia and Pacific Affairs, Iran

The reason and the need to take counter-terrorism measures is one of the most important and serious challenges facing this present world. This is the subject that is needed to be dealt with and resolved through an exchange of views and collaboration between all intellectuals and concerned personalities of all countries in the world. Through an exchange of views, followed by further efforts in enhancing cooperation for dealing with different forms of terrorism in the region and the world, we can overcome this newly emerged heinous phenomenon, preparing the ground for the establishment of sustainable stability and security in all countries in favour of our fellow human beings.

Developments and terror attacks that have taken place in the past years have proved the fact that the areas affected by this heinous phenomenon and its depth are far more than the previous assessment and judgement. In its form, terrorism has changed from a local and sectarian phenomenon to a regional and global one. Its essence has also been subject to some change and terror acts have been transformed from lower violence to ultra-violence, often ending in the most barbaric form. In the past, places where terrorism originated were few, but now we see a mushrooming of such places, to include Jakarta, Kabul, Paris, London, Madrid, Peshawar, Tunisia and many others—all being connected to each other.

Among the perpetrators of terror acts, a large number now are coming from Europe who have European accents and European origin. This by itself is proof to the claim that today, many parts of the world are facing this very serious threat. The key point in dealing with this phenomenon is the precise identification of its main root and causes. In this respect, some ideological factors in the Middle East as well as some acts of discrimination in Europe and the European failure and inability to absorb the marginalised populations leading to the latter's suppression, have provided the major and effective ground in order for more forces to join the radical group and factions.

If we have poverty as the ultimate cause of extremism in Africa, in Europe, liberalism, and along with it, globalisation, have not been able to act with success either. Therefore, it is necessary for us to identify, contain and eliminate all these factors that are giving rise to this phenomenon. In other words, instead of putting blame on other parties, levelling charges against others and being stranded on the identification level, we should look for a solution in favour of containment of this atrocious phenomenon. The Islamic Republic of Iran is one of the major victims of terrorism and is one of the forerunners in combating the same. To this end, it has taken successful action in this respect.

His Excellency Dr. Rouhani, the President of Islamic Republic of Iran, in his speech in 2013 in the UN General Assembly, proposed the idea of war against violence and extremism wave. That was welcomed by all member states and a relevant resolution on the same title was adopted unanimously. In his speech in 2015 in the UN General Assembly, President Rouhani, while emphasising the establishment of a united front against violent extremism, also proposed the adoption of a comprehensive plan of action for the same purpose.

In combating terrorism, double-standard policies will lead nowhere. We cannot on the one hand denounce terror groups and on the other, provide them with financial, logistical and intelligence support and even purchase goods and products from them. The terrorism that particularly spreads fear among people in all parts of the world poses serious intellectual and security threats to all people. In different deductions so far introduced by different parties, a few number of essential and significant misconceptions are visible that need to be attended and dealt with, and are as follows:

- Terrorism is not an asset but it is caused due to our collective failure. Any country that intends to invest in terrorism has to spend hundred times more to deal with its adverse consequences.
- Terrorism is parallel to the national interest—'flexible terrorism' and 'bad' or 'good' terrorism are nothing but words play. All extremist and terror schools of thought must be rejected, denounced and dealt with. Changing names and titles of terror groups and factions does not change the severity of their terror acts, nor does it change the essence of these groups. It must not be used as a reason to include or insert terrorists in new and different lists, differentiating them accordingly.
- Unfortunately, certain countries are trying to cover their political, economic or intelligence failures by fostering terrorists, little realising that as soon as such forces get strengthened, they start defining their own targets and those that have fostered such forces, will gradually not only lose their control over such groups, but they themselves will be turned into targets.
- Sometimes, the word terrorism is used to defame some groups or countries or tarnish the image of enemies in different disputes or conflicts. This has led to a sort of ambiguity in combating terrorism as well as an uncertainty in identifying the real terrorism. Such a cognitive deviation has now ended in an operational deviation in the fight against this heinous phenomenon.
- Islamic terrorism is a targeted and unforgettable ploy. It is possible that a Muslim with a perverted thinking commits a terror act under the influence of religion, just as it is possible

with every follower of any other religion. Islam, in its essence, is opposed to any act of terrorism. The Prophet of Islam was the prophet of mercy and he forgave all his enemies when the Muslims conquered Mecca. He forgave those enemies who had given their word to assassinate the Prophet of Islam. Therefore, Islamic terrorism is a wrongful expression that has been spread by the media.

- In the past, it was imagined that those crises triggered by the Taliban and the ISIS in a country will pose a primary challenge only to its neighbouring countries. Given the ubiquitous nature of terrorism, such postulation is not valid as terrorism can now impact all countries of the globe. This strengthens the need for cooperation among all countries in order to deal with the terror crisis.

In conclusion, I wish to raise some questions on the different dimensions of the acts of terror. The questions are:

- Can the terrorists push forward and implement their goals by themselves, without the support of some regional and international players?
- What ideologies are behind terror groups and which governments produce and support such ideologies?
- What are the major goals of the pro-terrorism governments and what are the main factors affecting other players to ignore the cooperation of certain countries with terror groups?
- Whether national interest can justify such actions?
- Which countries have benefited more from terror acts?

I believe that by finding answers to these questions, we can design the required operational mechanisms for seriously dealing with all terrorists.

PART II

CONTESTING THE SCOURGE

10

The Networks

P.C. Dogra

Terrorist networks, whether they are cooperative or adversarial, will certainly have important consequences for the people at large though it will make no difference to the number of ensuing fatalities. If they are cooperating, the massacres will of course be well planned and if they are opposed to each other, they will kill innocent people just to prove to each other that they are the dominant force. The only advantage in case they are adversaries is that intelligence machinery of the state can manage the access to the inner operative circle of the terrorist organisation. Cooperation or rivalry will also depend on the political goals of each group. Al-Qaeda has been encouraging cooperation between itself and the satellite terror groups. It has been having a number of allies and its global spread has been quite significant. Similar is the case of Hamas.

As on today Islamic state has emerged as a dominant terrorist organisation in the Middle East. There is a competition in carnage between the two outfits. Al-Qaeda has an unprecedented challenge from the Islamic State for leadership of the global jihadi movement. The attack on a Radisson Blu hotel in Bamako Mali just a week after the IS carnage in Paris which was claimed by al-Qaeda was obviously meant to assert its supremacy in the global jihad.

The origin of the Islamic State can be traced to a local affiliate of al-Qaeda in Iraq led by one Jordanian Abu Musab al-Zarqawi, its target being the U.S. troops. Later it started massacring the country's Shiite population. It resulted in tension between al-Qaeda and its affiliate as the former was opposed to al-Zarqawi's brutal attacks on Shias saying that it would turn Muslims against them. This friction was made public by the U.S. intelligence in 2005. In 2013, Abu Bakr al-Baghdadi renamed his terrorist group Islamic State (IS) as the Islamic State of Iraq and the Levant (ISIL), thus asserting his overall command and authority in Iraq and neighbouring Syria. Nusra Front, an al-Qaeda Syrian affiliate, rejected his claim and continued to swear allegiance to al-Zawahri. The other satellite terror groups which were the al-Qaeda satellites in Yemen and North Africa also did not accept the suzerainty of the ISIS and remained loyal to Al-Zawahri, with the result that by 2014, the Nusra Front and the Islamic State were fighting each other across northern Syria.

Both al-Qaeda and the IS want to completely obliterate Western influence in the Middle East and bring Muslims all over the world under a transnational caliphate governed by medieval version of Islamic law. But they are bitterly divided over strategy and leadership. Local al-Qaeda affiliates have sought to exploit and take advantage of the post-Arab spring turbulence. They put more emphasis on the issues related to the local people so as to ensure their support in their bid to uproot the monarchies. The Islamic State's strategy on the other hand, was to seize and then hold on to the land mass in Syria and Iraq. It declared a caliphate in 2014 and al-Baghdadi has proclaimed himself the leader of the Muslims all over the world. The split also echoed across the Muslim world i.e. Middle East and Africa by way of massacres.

So far, this rivalry between Islamic State and al-Qaeda, has been played out either in the Middle East or Africa. What we are concerned with is its impact in Afghanistan, Pakistan, India and Bangladesh. Of late, al-Qaeda has not been very active in South Asia, more so after the killing of Osama bin Laden. State aided terrorist outfits across the border in Pakistan have not so far accepted the dictates of Islamic State as they are the instruments of the State to launch low intensity proxy war in India and Afghanistan. Even in Kashmir, Pakistani proxy separatist leaders have declined to fall in line with the Islamic State. However, the IS Emir of Khurasan has claimed that very soon, Caliphate would be set up in Kashmir as also in Pakistan.

What could be the relationship of Tehrik-e-Taliban of Pakistan with the Islamic State or for that matter with Taliban of Afghanistan. Sunni terrorist outfits in Pakistan like Tehrik-e-Taliban Pakistan (TTP) have been killing Shia Muslims in Pakistan at regular intervals. With al-Qaeda's diminishing influence in Pakistan, will it result in Islamic State and TTP joining hands in Pakistan? What could be the impact of such a merger on the security environment in the Indian sub-continent?

An important issue which needs in-depth deliberation is the role of the Pakistan army. As of now, the Pakistan army is battling the TTP while at the same time extending support to and controlling the activities of those terrorist groups which it views as its strategic assets. Will it accept the Caliphate of Abu Bakar Al-Baghdadi? If not, will the TTP join hands with the Islamic State, accept Caliphate of Al Baghdadi and fight the Pakistan army jointly to establish the Sharia rule? How will such developments impact on the ongoing secessionist war launched by the Pakistani proxies in the Kashmir valley? Will the separatists stand up to the Islamic State or wilt and join its band wagon. The latter scenario will be quite a serious development.

11

Social Media, Technology and Terror

Manish S Sharma

As the Islamic State's forces were marching into Iraq's second largest city Mosul, after completely routing the U.S. trained Iraqi army, it made use of over 40,000 tweets in a single day, through a masterly use of hashtags. This strategy, therefore, indicates its focus on group messaging as well as branding concepts. Imagine the publicity it managed to generate for itself and its cause by a single victory that made perfect use of Social Media! The ISIS now rules an area almost as large as the territory of France. Now consider the fact that in only three months, since the end of October 2015, ISIS alone has claimed the responsibility of killing almost 500 people in strikes against France, Russia, Lebanon, Indonesia and recently in Damascus. And this is not counting casualties inflicted by its affiliates and other violent extremists in other parts of the world.

According to U.S. President Obama and UK Prime Minister Cameron, in all of this, technology and social media—Twitter, Facebook, Google, Apple, Microsoft, Yahoo, YouTube, WhatsApp, Skype, Tumblr, Instagram have actually become facilitators to the problem of global jihad.

An extremely critical issue involved in the use of social media and technology in the advancement of terror is that these new modes of communication respect no geographical or physical borders. There can thus be no border checks and controls to prevent the threat from entering any country. Consequently, every country is vulnerable to this grave threat. Hence, what we see unfolding, is a global war to dominate the narrative on the social media, the use of which has been perfected by the most barbaric and inhumane terror group of them all—The Islamic State (IS), also called Daesh or ISIS or ISIL (Islamic State of Syria/Islamic State of Syria and Levant). Several examples illustrate this fact, one of the earliest being the beheading of James Foley, the U.S. journalist on August 9, 2014, which was first widely seen on YouTube and then detailed tweets about the act were sent from ISIS sympathiser accounts in all parts of the world. Furthermore, the IS regularly uploads its digital magazine Dabiq (English language pdf) and distributes it on the social media, which then serves as a recruitment tool, a platform for spreading propaganda and provides sequential updates on recent happenings in the Caliphate. The magazine is also used to circulate religious arguments to justify its brutal tactics of slavery and other dehumanising acts. Another example of use of the social media has been by the Indonesian module of IS. This group used blog posts and mobile messaging apps extensively, to share and communicate its beliefs. As of now, it seems that the ISIS is winning hands down in this war between itself and the various governments fighting it (principally the U.S. government, but several others also) with respect to providing a counter narrative.

There are various ways in which the violent extremists and terrorists utilise the platform of social media to achieve various objectives. Let us examine some of these in greater detail:

- **Radicalisation**. This is done through a continuous process of indoctrination, spread of a particular ideology or use of false propaganda to further their cause.
- **Recruitment**. Some Twitter handles explain the entire process of recruitment in the ISIS and the way of life in the Caliphate so eloquently and convincingly, that it could put most professional marketeers to shame! A recent ISIS document available online has a list of Twitter accounts for male and female recruits, giving detailed instructions on how to avoid being detected by the LEA (local enforcement agencies), while

using social media.[1] Furthermore, recruitment films are recorded in many languages to serve an audience spread across several continents. In a recent example in India, a Hyderabad housewife, Afsha Zabeen alias Nicky Joseph, was performing two tasks. The first was enticing people to convert from Christianity to Islam and the second and more important one was spotting youngsters online who were responding to IS literature and lure them to join the group.

- **Initiating Calls for Action**. The social media is also used very effectively in co-ordinating attacks. On the mobile devices of several Paris attackers, encrypted apps for secret communications were found. Similarly in India, the National Investigation Agency (NIA) found this to be the case when they arrested 14 people for running ISIS modules across several cities and states in India.
- **Gathering Intelligence**. Some years ago, al-Qaeda recruited a Jordanian doctor, Humam al-Balawi, who actually served as a triple agent and organised a deadly attack on the CIA Khost base, killing several American operatives. Dr Humam al-Balawi was a quiet family man who was recruited and transformed into a terrorist on the web. In 2009, al-Balawi was recruited by Jordanian intelligence agents and then the CIA to infiltrate al-Qaeda's leadership in Afghanistan. Instead, al-Balawi duped his handlers and used his online credentials to establish contact with al-Qaeda and the Taliban, volunteering to carry out a suicide bombing. Seven American CIA officers and contractors, an officer of Jordan's intelligence service, and an Afghan working for the CIA were killed when al-Balawi detonated a bomb sewn into a vest he was wearing. Al-Balawi was not hiding his intentions or location. He was a fixture on message boards and even gave interviews to online propaganda magazines put out by al-Qaeda and the Taliban. He was actually telling people where he was and what he was going to do.[2]
- **Issuing Threats and Instilling Fear**. This is another way in which the social media is used by these groups. For instance,

at San Bernardino, California, after an incident in which 14 innocent Americans were shot dead by a Pakistani couple, several ISIS Twitter accounts spread the message—"California we have arrived...." This was posted from 335th Twitter account of Assamitri Media—a pro IS group.

- **Spread of false Propaganda and showing of Celebrations**. This is done through the use of beheadings to demean other religions and civilisations and spread religious hatred. ISIS now uses techniques borrowed from feature films and video games in its propaganda videos. In beheading videos, kidnappers announce the name of the next victim, enticing the viewer to stay tuned in, just like it happens on the reality TV shows.
- **Finances**. Finally, raising of finances is yet another purpose for which the ISIS and other groups use social media.

If we consider what is happening in India, the situation is no different, albeit only on a smaller scale. On 2 January 2016, a major terrorist attack was carried out on the Pathankot Air Force Station—one of India's most strategic assets. While the attackers were neutralised before they could destroy or damage aircraft and equipment, it was evident that the attackers had inside information. This was later confirmed with the arrest of an IAF technical engineer, Leading Air Craftsman (LAC) KK Ranjith, for supplying vital information to a woman with whom he got in touch through FaceBook. This woman, whose alias was Damini, while speaking to Ranjith, introduced herself as a media personnel working for a London based newspaper and spoke in UK accent through VOIP (Voice Over Internet Protocol).

The busting of different modules of the ISIS, first by the Delhi Police through raids and arrests starting in Uttarakhand, and subsequently by the National Investigation Agency across several states and cities, led to the arrest of 14 persons in pan Indian raids. The geographical spread of the locations shows the national reach that the terrorists have been able to develop. It needs to be emphasised that in both the above cases, the contact between recruiters and operatives were established through the social media platforms. The lead to NIA was also generated by the U.S. Central Intelligence Agency after coming across a FaceBook page of a person in Syria. It is believed that all the key masterminds of the plan and organisation had been in touch extensively through the use of technology—be it Janood-ul-Khalifa-e-Hind (an ISIS affiliated terror group in India), Mohammed Shafi Armar, who also goes by the name Yusuf-al-Hindi or Mudabbir Mushtaq Shaikh—the main handler who was co-ordinating with ISIS recruiters in Syria.[3]

Let us now examine as to what makes the social media into command and control networks of choice for the terrorists. The social media has certain inherent advantages over other forms of communication. It is cheap and very easily accessible, it facilitates quick, rapid and broad dissemination of information across wide swathes of geography throughout the world, in real time and it is a mode of unfettered communication without any kind of disturbances. Moreover, the ISIS and its sympathisers on the net are so dynamic, that they immediately create a new account even as one account is suspended by the parent social media company. The biggest advantage being that no matter where people are in the world, they can be connected instantly with others who sympathise with their cause. Thus, there are no borders in the realm of social media, unlike in the real world.

What can be done and what needs to be done to restrict the use of the social media by terrorist groups needs careful analysis and implementation. However, there are several problems faced by governments in countering the online terrorism menace/preventing misuse of social media. Every day we witness that the standard approaches to countering violent extremism online are lagging as new technology rises and is effectively made use of by the violent extremists. A major problem in India is the encryptions deployed by Apple, FaceBook, Google etc., that disallow law enforcement agencies to access the communications of a target. Servers of these companies are located outside India, so information is either not forthcoming or is vague in nature or it cannot be accessed in time. Moreover, there is no way to compel these companies to produce the information required. There is also a huge reluctance on the part of technology companies to share information speedily and do more to prevent incitement to violent extremism. Thus, at the moment, we seem to be technically incapable. What if the problem grows rapidly? To compound the problem, there is now a widespread and massive proliferation of fraudulent SIM cards issued on forged IDs. The department of telecommunications, instead of taking stringent action, only issues advisories to the Telecom Service Providers (TSPs)—and India being what it is—no action is initiated against TSPs. As of 2015 there were a total of 14,000 FIRs/complaints of forgery in getting SIM cards.[4]

When we look at the future and see the emerging threats, it can be seen that there have been several instances over the recent past wherein individuals, non state actors and even governments have made use of technology to inflict cyber warfare or cyber terrorism in some way. Let us consider some examples.

A computer virus named Stuxnet caused significant disruption to Iran's uranium enrichment programme by drastically altering the speed of centrifuges at its facility at Natanz. It is believed that this attack significantly delayed the capacity of Teheran to build nuclear weapons.[5] Then, on 15 August 2012, the computer network of Saudi Aramco was struck by a self-replicating virus that infected as many as 30,000 of its Windows based machines. Aramco took almost two weeks to recover from the damage. It is alarming that an attack of this scale was carried out against a company so critical to global energy markets. Later dubbed Shamoon, the virus caused significant disruption to the world's largest oil producer.[6] The Chinese too have been accused of cyber crimes. Recently, a US court charged 5 Chinese generals from the PLA and some other officers from Unit 61398 of cyber espionage against U.S. corporations by hacking websites and stealing information from major U.S. companies and then passing it on to Chinese companies.[7] Furthermore, reports indicate that Russia was able to successfully intercept a U.S. drone in Crimea by hacking into its controls. The drone was flying over the Crimea region of Ukraine in March 2014. It appears that hackers broke the connection between the drone and its operator using "complex radio-electronic technology".[8] It is believed that a number of states have military cyber-capabilities; and many of these can actually wage offensive cyber warfare. The possibility of proliferation of these capabilities is very real through co-operation of insiders with the violent extremists. It is within the realms of possibility that one day, a terrorist group could lay its hands on this arsenal and use it for attacking the infrastructure of a particular country. Similarly vulnerable, are the sectors in banking/financial industries, power grids, communication grids, schools, businesses, religious organisations, etc.. There are numerous other illustrations as well. In January 2012, tens of thousands of Israelis were the unwilling victims of 0xOmar, a hacker claiming to be a Saudi national whose plan was to use cyber terrorism in order to "hurt Israel—politically, economically and culturally," as the hacker wrote in an email exchange with an Israeli media source. The 0xOmar attacks targeted and exposed the personal and credit card data of Israelis on the web.[9] An al-Qaeda video calling for "electronic jihad" against infrastructure and other targets was shown by the FBI to the US House of Representatives' Homeland Security and Governmental Affairs Committee.[10] In yet another case, the Izz ad-Din al-Qassam cyber fighters launched 'Operation Ababil', a series of DDoS attacks against major banks in the West, which utilise Google cloud hosting, including Bank of America, Citigroup, Wells Fargo, BB&T and HSBC.[11] The possibilities of severe attacks by terrorists through cyber warfare are endless; operations that trigger a nuclear plant meltdown; operations that open a dam above a populated area causing destruction; operations that disable air traffic control resulting in airplane crashes. Therefore, a strong case needs to be made out with the Government of India for developing a separate, robust and continuously active Cyber Command, in the manner that the U.S. and China have done. The Chinese Central Military Commission (CMC) has on January 20, 2016, through a major military reform, centralised its space, cyber and information and electronic warfare forces, thus creating an efficient response system to handle any threats.[12]

Yet another major challenge confronting nations is the rapidly growing self-radicalisation that is taking place through the internet, without even a single physical preacher required. It is happening everywhere—from San Bernardino to Jakarta and from Haridwar to Hyderabad. Indian intelligence estimates that upwards of 25 Indian citizens have fought or are fighting in Syria, with 6 casualties as of January 2016.

So, what tools and resources should the Governments consider to respond to the problem? These can broadly be classified these into three segments. Firstly, deep collaboration and co-ordination with the private sector is necessary. Secondly, the international and national broadcasting arms of the government need a thorough overhauling, including on the social media and thirdly, a continuous and resolute engagement in counter propaganda efforts is required. All three have to be employed across three different sectors—military, intelligence and communication. In addition, the following are the other responses needed immediately:

- Extensive use of de-radicalisation techniques and methods to be employed by Governments.
- More effective monitoring of social media by governmental agencies is a must. For example, if the FaceBook account of the woman involved in San Bernardino attacks Tafshin Malik would have been monitored, it could have given indications about impending attacks/behaviour, enabling the security agencies to take appropriate counter measures in time.
- At the same time law enforcement agencies should use websites to elicit information by posing as sympathisers on a far more wider and frequent level than is being done now.
- Deployment of counter narrative propaganda/efforts/campaigns needs to be ensured in a manner more extensively and in a way that connects with vulnerable youngsters rather than appearing as simply yet another boring government effort.
- Initiating legal action against companies providing platform to IS and other similar organisations is necessary. December 2015 saw the introduction of a bipartisan bill co-sponsored by both Republicans and Democrats, in the U.S. Congress to compel companies to prevent online spread of hatred. In another recent example, an American serviceman's widow has

sued Twitter in the Federal court at Oakland, California, holding the company responsible for her husband's death in Iraq. It also needs to be made clear to companies that there are no technological issues that prevent them from doing more. Algorithms to prevent child pornography are already being used extensively.

- Effective and continuous international co-ordination between nation states in sharing intelligence, extradition of offenders and joint efforts in countering the propaganda. A recent example of such a collaboration came about when the CIA was tracking certain IP addresses of FaceBook users in Iraq and Syria in December 2015. The CIA found certain suspicious posts and shared the information with Indian intelligence in January. "7 Kalash Rakh Do" was the keyword, based on which extensive raids were conducted by the NIA, which led to the busting of several ISIS modules that were planning to execute terrorist attacks in India.
- Ensuring public and community participation in counter narrative efforts, through the involvement of leading and prominent figures who can have a huge influence on young, vulnerable and impressionable minds.
- Regular co-ordination among various government departments and agencies connected in some way with the internet and social media. Thus the NIA, ATS forces of all States, CERT, Department of Telecommunications and IT and the Telecom Regulatory Authority of India, all need to be on the same page as far as stopping the use of technology for propagating terrorism is concerned. Moreover, a working understanding and orientation towards common purpose of thwarting the nefarious designs of violent extremists is absolutely necessary between the Central Government and the State Governments. A stark reminder of this not being the case is the inability of India to create an effective National Counter Terrorism Centre, even though much smaller and less vulnerable countries have done so.
- The India heads of all technology companies need to be called

to discuss with the Government on terror related issues regularly so that both can arrive at an understanding on certain basic minimum requirements that companies need to follow to be in conformity with laws of India. The European Union has been doing this and there is no reason why we cannot. All companies need to show transparency and commit to national security.

- Developing a unique, universal, acceptable and enforceable identification system for the country is an immediate necessity which can prevent the huge misuse of fraudulent SIM cards.
- Finally, the immediate constitution of a National Security Advisory Board, which is the principal body of experts for advising the National Security Council and has been lying vacant for more than a year.

Finally, it needs to be said that our efforts to counter the aims of terrorists must, by its very nature, be democratic and dynamic. Democratic means involving community and religious leaders in counter narrative propaganda strategies and facilitating them to offer courses in schools that speak about the dangers of terrorism and provide the actual interpretation of religious scriptures instead of what is now widely preached as the interpretation. This would also help generate feedback from the citizens and increase their willingness to be forthcoming with information. The efforts need also to be dynamic by having the ability to adapt and evolve to changing situations and environment in terms of technology and surveillance software. What is needed is a firm resolve on the parts of the various governments, private companies, the media and the society at large to deprive the jihadists and proponents of violent extremism, of the virtual territory that they seek to dominate, just as we deny them the occupation of physical/geographic space.

For us in India, the most effective way of taking the fight back to the violent extremists is the start of an unprecedented co-operation between all major political parties on the issue of national security, regardless of their political ideology. This would set the national discourse and send a strong signal to the terrorists and their backers. A recent example is the law passed by the U.S. Congress on December

15, 2015, which required private companies to report online terrorist activity. The bill was co-sponsored by both Republicans and Democrats. Perhaps, now is the time for a transformation of India's political landscape by introducing a comprehensive law to deal with terrorism and the use of social media to promote terrorism.

ENDNOTES

1. Presley Thomas, "Not Just Twitter: How IS is using Social Media Apps to Recruit in India", *The Hindustan Times*, January 25, 2016
2. Evan Kohlmann, *Flashpoint Global Partners*, New York Quoted by Gina Vergel of Fordham University
3. Rajshekhar Jha, "CIA leads help Indian agencies bust ISIS cells", *The Times of India*, January 23, 2016
4. Ankur Sirothia, "Retail counters prone to SIM cards misuse on fake ID", *The Times of India*, September 3, 2015
5. Mark Clayton, "Stuxnet attack on Iran nuclear program came about a year ago, report says", *The Christian Science Monitor*, January 3, 2011
6. Christopher Bronk, Eneken Tikk-Ringas, "The Cyber Attack on Saudi ARAMCO", *Survival: Global Politics and Strategy, International Institute of Strategic Studies*, pp. 81-96 April–May 2013
7. "U.S. Charges Five Chinese Military Hackers for Cyber Espionage Against U.S. Corporations and a Labor Organization for Commercial Advantage", May 19, 2014, *Justice News*, US Department of Justice
8. Isaac R. Porsche III, "Cyberwarfare Goes Wireless", *US News World Report*, April 4, 2014
9. Housien Couriel Deborah, "The Evolving Law on Cyber Terrorism: Dilemmas in International Law and Israeli Law", *International Institute for Counter Terorism*, IDC Herzlia, March 23, 2013
10. Jack Cloherty, "Virtual Terrorism: Al-Qaeda Video Calls for 'Electronic Jihad'", *ABC News*, May 22, 2012
11. Nicole Perlroth and Quentin Hardy, "Bank Hacking Was the Work of Iranians, Officials Say", *The New York Times*, January 8, 2013
12. John Costello, "China Finally Centralizes Its Space, Cyber, Information Forces", *The Diplomat*, January 20, 2016.

12

Life Blood of Terrorism: Deciphering the Challenge

Colonel Vivek Chadha

Terrorism is widely considered as one of the major threats facing the world at large. While this reality gained credence after 9/11, the emergence of Islamic State (hereafter referred to as the Daesh), further reinforced the transnational impact of the group. Amongst the important factors which allow such groups to conduct their violent actions, is the sustained supply of money to fund their activities. This not only allows terror groups to undertake individual strikes against hapless citizens and non-combatants, it also facilitates the smooth functioning of large organisational structures of these groups. In fact, it is a well established reality that in contrast to the funding for individual attacks, it is the day to day running of terrorist organisations that demand the bulk of monetary resources.

This paper attempts to elaborate on the different models of terror funding prevalent amongst major groups as well as smaller entities in order to better understand the challenges involved in neutralising them. The models vary from full-spectrum to foreign sponsored and limited funding to self funded mechanisms adopted by terrorist groups. An assessment of these models highlights the challenges associated with the wide ranging method of funding and the need for enhancing the international efforts to fight the contagion. It also emerges that often, narrow perceived strategic interests of individual countries, constrain the larger effort to fight terrorism and the financing of terrorism, especially given the transnational nature of the emerging threat.

Sources of Terror Funds

Over a period of time, terrorist groups have employed a variety of methods to raise funding and transfer the proceeds. There are different methods of categorising terror funding. One amongst these is to divide it between internal and external sources of funds. These can further be classified on the basis of sources. As an illustration, external funds can emanate from individual donations, state sponsorship, narcotics, non-governmental organisations, counterfeit currency amongst others. Internal funds can be raised from taxation of locals and extortion of businesses, drug trafficking and crime. These funds can be transferred primarily through four means to include cash, trade, hawala and legal mechanisms. Legal systems could include banks, money transfer service schemes, prepaid cards etc.

Terror groups can not only have multiple sources of terror funding, they can also exploit various combinations to include both internal and external sources. They can also employ more than one means of transferring funds based on the limitations observed in the defensive mechanisms, functioning in different countries that are being targeted.

Case Study: Daesh

Daesh has emerged as one of the wealthiest terrorist groups in the world. While there have been fluctuating estimates in terms of the resources at its disposal, recent indicators suggest that it could have a monthly income of approximately $80 million.

Proceeds from the groups initial foray into captured areas yielded a substantial amount from banks and treasuries that were taken over. They also raised significant amounts from sale of artefacts from centuries old archeological sites that were smuggled out from the region, only to be sold in the lucrative markets of the West. This was supplemented with large volumes of oil exports, which were the highest during the initial period of occupation of mineral rich areas that were the target of Daesh operations. The income from oil has often been estimated to contribute most to the funding of the group. However, recent measures seem to have adversely affected the ability of the group to extract and sell oil, especially to foreign buyers. In a bid to minimise the revenues generated from oil, air strikes have had a salutary impact. "As long as they control territory, the question becomes not how do you stop them from producing, but how do you make sure that for the interim period they still hold territory, that they derive as little profit as possible from oil, and minimise their ability to use it in their governance." Oil sales have also been hit by lowering of international crude oil prices, which has made the smuggling of oil to other countries unviable to the extent it was earlier. Further, pressure has built up on neighbouring countries to place curbs on export of oil through their territory.

Besides oil, a large percentage of revenues of the group also comes from taxation of services to the people living in areas under its control. This includes large territories in eastern Syria and northwestern Iraq. In these areas, the Daesh is practically running a parallel government with all elements of a state, at least in terms of the administration of occupied areas. Documents emerging from the region suggest that the local population is paying taxes on provision of electricity and waste disposal facilities, transfer of money, income, business produce, movement of goods and vehicles etc. Daesh has also received some contributions from foreign donors.

Daesh has employed methods like kidnapping for ransom as a means of raising of funds as well. In 2014, the amount collected is estimated to be approximately $45 million. There have been a number of cases wherein, foreigners of different nationalities have been kept hostage and released on payment of hefty ransom amounts. While a number of countries refute this allegation, which is also contrary to international guidance on the subject, however, there is adequate circumstantial evidence which points in this direction.

Funding for the group has also been generated through donations from sympathetic contributors from the Arab world as well as the

West. In addition to more traditional means of appealing to contributors, advances in technology, including social media has been exploited by the Daesh to raise funds. Twitter, Skype and other messaging services have been employed to provide directions and aid to contribute funds. An incident of a volunteer who attempted to support the cause of Daesh by helping raise funds for the group illustrates the case. He stated that "money is the largest resource for extremists and people should fight with their money as well as with their bodies and words. He urged people to donate money, often times a third of their salary, as it is considered a type of jihad. These tweets would sometimes list specific weapons and the amount needed to purchase them. One example included asking for specific cash donations of 5,000 USD from each family."

A large percentage of Daesh money gets transferred in the form of cash. This provides the easiest method for moving money without major use of the legal financial system, which can trace and track movement of electronic trails. Incidents of foreign fighters and sympathisers carrying cash during their travel to the region have come to light, which not only reinforce this method of moving money, but also the source of some of the funding of the group.

A passenger from EU member state arrived in Istanbul's Sabiha Gokcen Airport with four large pieces of luggage and two sports bags. Upon suspicion by the competent authorities at the airport, he was interviewed and found to be in possession of 3,500 Euro. The passenger stated that he was visiting and would go back to his homeland in a weeks' time. Upon search of his luggage, many pairs of tracking boots, jeans, ISIL labelled t-shirts and sweatshirts and torches were found. He was denied entry and was added to the Turkish no-entry list.

The different methods employed by the group for raising and transferring money, suggests that Daesh follows a full spectrum funding and transfer system. This includes almost every potential source, both internal and external, to raise funding, as well as the means available for transferring it. The multiplicity of methods employed provides an inherent resilience to the group against pressure on specific sources. The recent instance of the group reducing the payments of its cadres to fifty per cent, possibly as a result of low oil prices and targeting of its wells and refineries suggests that other means like extortion and taxation continue to sustain the terror group.

It is also evident from available documentation, that Daesh could not have supported the scale of funding it generates, without foreign support. In this instance, especially in case of oil exports, the possibility of a substantial percentage of oil moving through Turkey, across the borders of both Iraq and Syria has come to light. Similarly, given the need for oil, even rebel groups which are otherwise fighting Daesh, have bought oil from the group, possibly based on a decision purely guided by economic considerations. This more than reinforces the concept of the economy of terrorism that tends to flourish in areas where terrorist groups and middlemen extract their share of revenue from the money which flows into an area to fight terrorism itself.

Case Study: Lashkar-e-Taiba

The Lashkar-e-Taiba (LeT), is amongst the most lethal and well funded terror groups in South Asia. While it was created to focus its acts of terrorism on J&K and thereafter India, however, over a period of time, its reach and impact has moved beyond the Indian shores. The LeT recruits its cadres primarily from the jihadi factories of Pakistan with an aim of pursuing its strategic objectives in the sub-conventional domain. The volunteers are provided basic and advanced training, in accordance with their assigned roles and end up as the instrument of proxy war inside India. Amongst the most sensational strikes by LeT cadres was the 26/11 terrorist attack in Mumbai. This not only brought to the fore the reach and impact of the group, but also its ability to finance an elaborate operation which needed substantial funding.

The LeT's funding flows through two distinct channels. This includes direct support provided to the group as also through the Jamaat-ud-Dawa (JuD), which operates as an NGO, even as it provides a front for fund collection of the LeT. This enlarges the scope of funding of the group beyond the terror activities of LeT to welfare activities like the post-earthquake initiatives taken by them. While some funds collected are utilised for welfare activities, a percentage is funnelled for terrorism in the name of jihad. The dubious role of the JuD has been highlighted through classified U.S. government reports leaked in the past. It suggests that "Some of JuD's budget, using funds raised both from willing donors and by fraud, is dedicated to social services or humanitarian relief projects, while some is used to finance LeT operations." This provides a degree of legitimacy, despite international designation of both as terrorist organisations, amongst the support base of the group within the country. As a result, a large percentage of funding of the group emanates from donations from the local people, as well as supporters settled in Europe, West Asia and the U.S.A. Some of the activities for raising donations continue, despite a ban in as obvious a method as placement of donation boxes outside shops in the open market. This not only indicates wide support for the group in certain areas of the country, but also the blind eye being turned by government agencies.

Besides this support base, the LeT and JuD also run legitimate businesses, which raise funds for their activities. Amongst the most lucrative means employed by the group to raise funds is the sale of animal skins donated by people during the festival of Eid-al-Adha. With an average price of $50 for each skin sold, an estimated 1000,000 pieces were sold by the group in 2013, which gives an idea of the money raised in the process. The group also maintains fish farms and sells carpets as part of its legitimate business interests.

The LeT functions as an extension of the state apparatus. This is reinforced by their not only receiving funds directly from the Punjab government on at least two occasions that have been documented in the garb of welfare funds for the JuD, but also by the ISI to conduct specific operations, as confirmed by David Headley, while deposing in the U.S. State connivance with actions of the LeT, has also been confirmed by him as part of his deposition to a Mumbai court in relation to the 26/11 investigations. The ISI also employs the proceeds of fake Indian currency notes (FICN) that it pushes inside India, as well as drug money to fund its underground activities, of which the LeT is a major part.

Past instances indicate that the LeT has employed various means to transfer these funds. While cash collections are the most important method utilised to collect resources within the country, it has also used the legal channel and trade for transferring funds. However, in case of its activities in India, hawala remains possibly the most effective and efficient method for moving money, without the accompanying threat of monetary trails accompanying it.

Case Study: Indian Mujahideen

The Indian Mujahideen (IM), draws its roots from the Students Islamic Movement of India (SIMI), since most of its initial cadre base were active members of SIMI, prior to their making the shift towards an overtly violent terrorist organisation. The group came into prominence in 2007, with the initiation of a series of terror strikes inside India. Their usefulness to the cause of Pakistani establishment's aim of destabilising India became evident when a part of its leadership shifted base to Pakistan. However, their activities received a setback after the arrest of a number of their senior cadre.

The IM, when compared with both the IS and LeT, has a modest reach, impact and funds at their disposal. As a result of this, their initiation into terrorism was accompanied by funding through criminal activities, which included looting of banks, businesses and kidnapping for ransom. As an example, "Several operatives like Noor@Anwar and Abdul Wahid@Khan continued to stay in the UAE, in order to collect and supply funds to the field operatives. The absconding accused Amir Reza Khan continued to collect money for the IM through extortion from businessmen and received an amount of about Rs 10 crore in 2010, when he participated in the extortion from Kolkata in India." However, their employment by the ISI as a proxy tool against India, led to direct state sponsored funding emanating from Pakistan. More recent evidence suggests that the IM has received most funds through money transfer service schemes (MTSS), which include money transfer through alternate legal agencies like the Western Union. In order to ensure security, transfers were initiated in favour of either fake accounts or those of sympathisers and subsequently handed over to the IM cadre.

Case Study: Limited Funding Attacks

The world was shaken up by the attacks in Paris on the office of Charlie Hebdo. The attacks were carried out to punish the cartoonists at the magazine office who were seen as indulging in blasphemous actions by the attackers, in light of their cartoons of Prophet Mohammed. The resultant attack led to the death of 12 people. Amongst the attackers, Said and Cherif Kouachi indicated a linkage with al-Qaeda in Arabian Peninsula (AQAP).

The funding for the attack came from three sources. Some funds were provided by AQAP. In addition, sale of counterfeit goods and personal sources of the gunmen provided the rest of the funding for the attack. This was done by trading in of a car and raising a loan. "Cherif Kouachi is also said to have received $20,000 from AQAP before leaving Yemen, and fellow terror cell member Amedy Coulibaly purchased several of the weapons used during the attacks drawing from a $7,000 personal loan and possibly by trading in a car. Weapons possessed by the Kouachi brothers and Coulibaly had a reported street value of 27,000 euros."

Case Study: Self-Funded Attacks

On May 3, 2015, in Garland Texas, a terror strike was attempted by two U.S. nationals. Nadir Soofi and Elton Simpson decided to strike at the Prophet Mohammed cartoon competition. The shooters were, however, intercepted by a vigilant police officer and brought down before they could cause any fatalities in the area. According to investigative reports that emerged after the incident, the two gunman had been enraged by what they considered blasphemous activity and wanted to seek retribution for the same. Just prior to the incident, they had indicated their allegiance to the Daesh in a twitter message.

Investigations into the incident revealed that the two had raised funding primarily from their own sources. This included overdraft facilities, loans and personal savings. This was used by the attackers to purchase the weapons needed, in this case rifles to carry out the attack. This was evidently facilitated by the sale of small arms with relative ease in the U.S. as compared to most other countries.

Assessment of Sources

The five case studies present a wide variety of funding patterns, with each having its distinct characteristics. The Daesh model is primarily based on the exploitation of its ground holding role, which is the closest to creation of a state model. This allows it to not only extract the resources available in this region varying from oil to artefacts, but also facilitates taxation and extortion of the local people and businesses. A mix of support from tribal areas that supported the military actions of the Daesh in the wake of the perceived threat of Shia domination after the overthrow of Saddam and employment of terror as the basis for enforcing its will, has led to the success of this model. It has further been supplemented by the support of external actors, without which a large percentage of oil sales across borders could not have materialised. Given the wide ranging options available to Daesh to fund its organisation and operations, the model remains reasonably resilient till the time sale of oil can continue and the group holds large swathes of territory which lends itself to raising financial resources. However, this strength of the group could also become a limitation in case their hold shrinks over the region and external financial support, which forms a limited percentage of their budget, is inadequate to support their operations. If one was to compare this model with others in the past, it can possibly be related to the Taliban. They too succeeded, through the control of territory, in funding their large organisational structure as well as operations, accompanied by state support from Pakistan. The differentiating factor relates to the Daesh emerges as a more sophisticated user of technology and the level to which they have been able to take their funding campaign, incorporating the best of modern communication technologies.

The LeT emerges as a very well funded terror organisation, which like the Daesh relies more on domestic resources for raising funds. However, unlike the Daesh, it is not a quasi-state structure, but more an extension of the intelligence apparatus of a state, Pakistan. Its funding is primarily raised through donations in the form of direct contributions from supporters within the country, though a percentage also comes from abroad. However, unlike the Daesh, the Pakistani state also funds the group, both through direct and public funding of the JuD, as well as more clandestine means as in case of the ISI. Similarly, since the LeT funding is based more on voluntary support within Pakistan, the resilience and consistency of the sources remains more robust and is likely to be sustained over a longer period of time. Just as the Daesh sustenance is based primarily on its ability to control territorial areas in Iraq and Syria, the LeT's ability is dependent on the continued support of the Pakistani state.

The IM is a much smaller group in comparison, with a limited support base in India. However, its adoption by the ISI dictates its renewed ability to fund its organisational structure and operations. Unlike its past attempts to raise funds through kidnapping and other crimes, a large proportion of its funds emanates from Pakistan. Therefore, the IM too owes its continued ability to sustain its organisational structure to its support from the ISI. This deep reliance is likely to ensure that the IM will function as a tool of proxy war for Pakistan.

The Charlie Hebdo attack suggests that a small group of radicalised volunteers, who may be separated by thousands of miles from the nerve centre of a terrorist group, can be supported in part through funding. While this provides the principal corpus, it can further be supplemented by individuals raising funds through various self-financing options as seen in this case. This form of contributory funding effort is best suited for remotely coordinated and motivated attacks and can possibly become a model for future attacks in areas far removed from West Asia and Northern Africa. Europe can potentially be affected the most by this form of funding and attacks.

Self-financed attacks like the one witnessed in Texas, may have limitations given the constraints on sources of funding. However, in a country like the U.S., where access to automatic weapons is easier and limited funding can cater to its procurement, such attacks cannot be ruled out. The linkage of such attacks to groups like the Daesh provide them with the requisite publicity and the notion of a virtual reach, which may be difficult to achieve in reality. It is possibly for this reason that the Daesh has attempted to publicise and encourage lone wolf attacks on targets in the west.

Conclusion

The trends of terror funding suggest that terrorists have succeeded in remaining a step ahead of intelligence and enforcement agencies in most countries. This is reinforced by the wide spread and varied form of funding that has successfully supported organisational structures of groups as elaborate as the Daesh and Taliban, as well as smaller cells, which emerge in order to conduct a strike, irrespective of the individual cost to the attackers.

It is evident that funding can be internal to a region or country, as also external. It is the challenge of external funding which relates it to transnational monetary systems, as also transit of cash and goods. It is evident that narrow strategic gains and perceived national interests of countries at times lead to these systems being exploited. The gaps in existing international structures and frameworks are capitalised by terrorist groups to fund their activities. The purchase of oil by rival terror groups fighting the Daesh emerges as a functional requirement, however, its trade and transit through neighbouring countries, can only indicate short term gains at the heavy cost of human suffering in the region. While this paper does not touch upon weapon trafficking and its sale to terror groups, however, it remains yet another example of middlemen, traders and countries benefitting at the cost of sustenance of terrorist organisations like the Daesh.

The variety of funding patterns and geographical spread of attacks suggests that no region of the world is safe from terrorism and can potentially contribute to its funding as well. In a number of cases like the sale of counterfeit goods, as highlighted in one of the case studies, it emerges that crime and terrorism have been and remain closely interlinked. Therefore, even as steps are initiated to fight the financing of terrorism, its linkage with crime must simultaneous be investigated to better understand existing networks. This raises the need for an approach which is not constrained by a narrow perspective of terror funding. Instead, there is a need for enlarging its scope to include linkages with crime and money laundering.

13

Terrorist Infrastructure and Financing

Amit Kumar

This paper delves into the topic of terrorist infrastructure and financing.

First, terrorist financing includes the setting up of terrorist infrastructure and not just the costs incurred in perpetrating terrorist attacks. In fact, financing is very much a part of the terrorist infrastructure. Terrorist infrastructure includes the costs incurred in radicalisation, training, travel, procuring weapons, running effective media campaigns and IT infrastructure, upkeep and maintenance of terrorist group members, and lastly, the costs of perpetrating terrorist attacks.

Second, terrorists succeed by moving men, money, materiel, and messages—often collectively, called 'material support'. For the purposes of this paper, terrorist infrastructure will be used interchangeably with terrorist financing or material support.

Third, lone wolves or terrorist group inspired attacks are just the ultimate perpetration or the delivery mechanism for a terrorist enterprise that has been financed to indoctrinate, radicalise, and train terrorists, a key part of the terrorist infrastructure as mentioned earlier.

Fourth, the motivations of donors determine the financing activity of terrorist organisations. For example, the motivations of donors in the Afghan War of the 1980s was anti-Soviet; the motivations of the Afghan War post 9/11 was anti-U.S. led coalition, and the motivations of donors contribution to the South Asian terrorist groups is anti-India. Similarly, the motivations of donors contributing to the financing of terrorist organisations in the Middle East were anti-U.S., during the War in Iraq since 2003. The motivations of donors financing ISIS have been anti-Assad and anti-Shia. Donors give funds to appease certain domestic constituencies in their home countries, e.g. donors from states in the Middle East.

Fifth, the profile of donors additionally impacts the financing of terrorist infrastructure. Rich donors usually are fewer in number and give money in larger amounts compared to the large number of unwitting donors who give in much smaller amounts.

Sixth, the motivations of terrorist groups also affect their financing. In South Asia, the terrorist groups are anti-Soviet, anti-US led coalition in Afghanistan as well as anti-India; in the Middle East, they are anti-Soviet, anti-U.S., anti-Shia, pro-territory governance (e.g. ISIS) and pro-regional and global caliphate (again ISIS).

Seventh, terrorists raise and move money through cash couriers, charities, illicit business fronts, hawala, trade based money laundering (TBML), state support, and through formal banking channels. The use of banking channels for terrorist financing is exemplified by HSBC's correspondent banking relationship with terrorist financing tainted Al-Rajhi Bank[1] in Saudi Arabia and Islami Bank in Bangladesh respectively. Certain countries also serve as transit points for flow of terrorist funds, namely Iran in the Middle East and Sri Lanka and Maldives in South Asia.

Eight, the direction of flow of funds and fighters is also an important aspect of terrorist financing. Fighters from the Gulf states joined the Afghan war against the Soviet Union; fighters from South Asia went to Iraq and Syria to join ISIS. Lashkar-e-Taiba (LeT) has Saudi connections; the Taliban has Qatari connections.

Nine, another significant feature of terrorist financing activity are the Terrorist Financing Facilitation Networks. The pre-established channels of financial support from previous wars are very much intact in the current terrorist financing ventures. The Gulf-Pak-Afg financial pipeline of terrorist financing flows is still intact, as is the illegal sale of opium from Afghanistan that generates revenues for the Taliban and its operations. The Role of D-Company in drug trafficking and laundering the proceeds of this trade, thus acting as a terrorist financing facilitation network, is worth noting. All groups in the South Asian terrorist networks, live in relative harmony and recognise the predominance of the Afghan Taliban. India's relatively porous borders with its neighbours facilitate the flow of terrorists, money, criminals, drugs, fake Indian currency notes (FICN), arms, etc. According to some media reports, the D-Company–Boko Haram nexus has been developing since 2014, thus showing that strong intra-regional linkages may also facilitate the financing of terrorist infrastructures. A fact that cannot be underscored enough, is the presence in large numbers of South Asian expatriates in Gulf countries, thus boosting the intra-regional linkages that may be exploited by terrorist financiers to route their funds to organise, plan, and perpetrate terrorist attacks. For the Middle East, the terrorist financing facilitation networks are:

- The pre-established channels of financial support from previous wars that are very much intact.[2]
- The Illegal sale of oil from Iraq and Syria and the role of oil brokers and smugglers in oil smuggling.
- Ingratiation of local inhabitants in Iraq by ISIS, to gain their support.
- The predominance of ISIS amongst terrorist groups, since it enjoys funds, familiarity with terrain, and the confidence of fighters and the ability to co-opt smaller competitors.
- The porous borders between Iraq and Syria and between Syria and Turkey that facilitate flow of money, terrorists, criminals, arms, oil, etc.
- The ISIS-Boko Haram material support and information technology support relationship.

Ten, the efficacy of terrorist financing networks is also an interesting feature. One metric of testing efficacy, is the achievement of the objectives of donors of terrorist funds and their recipients, namely the terrorist groups. The al-Qaeda-Taliban combine was successful in driving the Soviet Forces and almost the entire US-led coalition from Afghanistan in the Afghan war of the 1980s and the more recent post 9/11 war in Afghanistan respectively. Another metric is the fact that terrorist groups are flush with funds, despite the vigorous efforts to counter their financing. Thus, terrorist financing networks are resilient to withstand the Countering the Financing of Terrorism (CFT) and Counter Terrorism (CT) measures as evidenced by the ready availability of funds with the Taliban in South Asia and ISIS in the Middle East respectively, despite the implementation of CFT measures against these terrorist groups. As charities started getting listed by the U.S. and UN, post 9/11, terrorist organisations modified their terrorist activity from that of raising and moving money through listed charities to that of using trusts in mosques, and moving cash through cash couriers across porous borders. The Afghan Taliban used fake identities to own and operate bank accounts of charities in Pakistan. Fleeing Taliban operatives withdrew cash and carried it to Pakistan and to the Taliban embassies in the Gulf. For the Middle East, achievement of objectives of donors and recipients in the earlier Iraq war can be measured by the fact that the US led coalition had to leave Iraq. In the current ISIS scenario, one can see the achievement of objectives of recipients in terms of ISIS creating an active terrorist group with international reach. However, the donors' objective of the removal of Assad through ISIS has been belied. ISIS as a terrorist group is flush with funds, which shows that the goal of the recipients, i.e. ISIS has been achieved. The ISIS led TF networks in the Middle East are resilient to withstand CFT and CT measures. Another factor that facilitates the success of these TF networks is the use cash couriers, cash transactions, barter, laundering mechanisms to move proceeds of the sale of smuggled oil, etc.

Eleven, CFT Measures used are of four type; Sanctions, Investigations and Enforcement, Regulation, and Outreach. Sanctions have a useful name and shame deterrence element as displayed by freezing of assets of tainted charities, and illicit business fronts by the U.S.; however most countries other than the U.S. have not followed suit in actually freezing assets of U.S. and UN listed entities. Also, many other non-U.S. jurisdictions lack the political will and/ or technical capacity to freeze assets of listed individuals and entities. Another problem is that once sanctioned, these organisations modify their names to escape being sanctioned; in other words the successor organisations of these sanctioned organisations can no longer be designated or be susceptible to assets freeze sanctions measures. Outreach efforts made by the U.S. to South Asian countries have had mixed results, due to lack of political will and/or technical capacity and/or corruption in a number of these countries. Outreach to Gulf states has been aggressive, but political will amongst these states to tackle funding of terrorist groups outside their states has been lacking. Regulations to counter terrorist financing are hampered by the lack of adequate laws against TF through cash couriers and charities; also, the concept of material support in these countries is not as extensive and exhaustive as it is in the U.S. Investigations and enforcement actions are hamstrung by historically weak investigatory capacities in South Asian and Middle Eastern states that are now improving in some jurisdictions; again, very few TF convictions and prosecutions result from such investigations of terrorist financing cases, which again puts a question mark over effectiveness of implementation and impact of CFT measures.

Twelve, some important takeaways for CFT Policy are:

- South Asian TF networks rely on funding from the Gulf.
- Porous borders result in flow of funds and fighters.
- Criminal groups aid and abet terrorist financing;
- Al-Qaeda's call for a South Asian branch is to ensure that Gulf donors do not lose interest in South Asia, now that U.S. led troops are exiting Afghanistan.
- Quite notably, the killing of terrorist financiers does not kill the TF networks.
- Also, South Asian and Middle East CFT networks are connected.

For Middle Eastern Terrorist Financing Networks, the key takeaways for CFT policy are:

- Middle Eastern TF networks rely on funding from the Gulf and Turkey.
- Porous borders result in flow of funds and fighters.
- Criminal groups aid and abet terrorist financing.
- ISIS is attracting most of the funds from the Gulf, now that it is a successful terrorist organisation and the al-Nusra Front (ANF) is only a variant of ISIS, as both of these terrorist organisations are al-Qaeda affiliated.
- Killing of terrorist financiers does not kill the TF networks.

Finally, the best CFT measures against South Asian terrorist financing networks are:

- Curtailing TF funding from the Gulf through sanctions, especially their implementation across South Asian and Gulf States.
- Enforcing Stricter border control measures.
- Doing More aggressive outreach with South Asian States.
- Clamping down on operatives of the D-Company including by extradition and by enforcing Mutual Legal Assistance Treaties (MLAT) as well as by designations, seizures, and arrests.
- Ensuring that banks in South Asia implement more stringent CFT controls.
- Making sure that U.S. security interests are squared with U.S. diplomatic interests.
- Cooperating with India on CFT, especially in intelligence sharing and law enforcement collaboration.
- Exercising greater controls on on-line recruitment and fund raising.
- Initiating greater outreach to worship places and involving the religious minority in the condemnation of al-Qaeda and Associated South Asian Groups' ideology and tactics.

Similarly for Middle Eastern terrorist financing networks, the best CFT measures are:

- Curtailing TF funding from the Gulf through sanctions, especially their implementation across Gulf states and Turkey.

- Stricter border control measures.
- The continuation of aggressive outreach with Gulf states and Turkey.
- The clampdown on smugglers and oil dealers engaged in black marketing including through arrests, seizures, designations.
- Ensuring that banks in the Gulf and Turkey implement more stringent AML/CFT controls.
- Making sure that U.S. security interests are squared with U.S. diplomatic interests.
- Conducting thorough vetting of Free Syrian Army (FSA) recruits, as many of them have been co-opted by ISIS.
- Exercising greater controls on on-line recruitment and fund raising.
- Initiating greater outreach to worship places and involving the religious minority in condemnation of ISIS ideology and tactics.

ENDNOTES

1. Al-Rajhi Bank is mentioned as part of Usama Bin Laden's Golden Chain of twenty largest donors in documents seized by investigators.
2. The Initial pathway of financial support to the predecessor of ISIS, Al-Qaida in Iraq (AQI) was through Syria.
3. Between 1988 and 2001, 30,733 lives had been lost to terrorism in J&K. "Fatalities in Terrorist Violence – 1988-2017", *South Asia Terrorism Portal*, http://www.satp.org/satporgtp/countries/india/states/jandk/data_sheets/annual_casualties.htm

14

Evolution and Innovation

Lt. Col. (Res.) Uri Ben Yakov

This paper will focus on the evolution we have identified in terror organisations, innovations which have influenced their financial sources and the ways they transfer money. In conclusion, I will share my thoughts on how I propose we combat these innovations.

The first innovation is the rise in what we call hybrid terror organisations. An additional innovation is the structure of terror organisations. The third innovation deals with terror organisation's extensive use of the cyber world, a world which utilises all aspects of terror.

A hybrid terror organisation is not a new phenomenon, though the global jihad has taken the idea one step further, as we will see in the case study regarding ISIS. The most important characteristic of a hybrid terror organisation is the control over territory and the population within it, both of which facilitate independence in funding its activities. The fact that the hybrid organisation has a military wing is clear—without such a wing it would not be a terror organisation. However, it also includes a political and/or social wing.

Independent funding may be sourced in criminal activity, something which we are familiar with even from non-hybrid organisations. However, hybrid organisations are less exposed, as they can carry out said criminal activity in the territory under its control. Another source of independent funding is legitimate business or investments. This is also not exclusive to hybrid organisations. The source of independent funding which is unique to hybrid organisations is the taxes drawn from the population in the areas under the organisation's control; personal, business and other types of taxes—just like in established countries. Another source of funding unique to hybrid organisations is the use of natural resources present in the territory under its control. It is important to remember that the sources of independent funding mentioned, are all in the territory under the hybrid organisation's control, as are the money and the transfer of funds.

Let us move on to the second innovation which I would like to discuss, the transformation in the structure of terror organisations. This will allow us to see how these changes have influenced fund raising. The traditional organisation structure is the hierarchal model we all know. There are many diverse structures and I shall not analyse all of them, but I shall present two as examples: the 'Hub', in which the leader has exclusive access to each of the network's activists, and the 'Chain', in which each member in the network is connected to only two other members. However, the structure which interests us the most is one in which all have access to all, a structure which fits the internet's infrastructure.

Let us now examine the meaning of the innovations/ evolutions which we see in organisational structure, in relation to terror fundraising. In the traditional hierarchal model, the donators transferred the money to the fund-raisers, who passed it on to the organisation's financial centre, from where it was later given to the activists and terror cells. In the case of a hybrid organisation, the money is also given to the civilian population as public goods.

In the new structural model, in which everyone is connected to everyone, we can see that at times the donator transfers the money directly to the end user, the activists/ terror cells. In actuality, there are organisations which make use of only the traditional ways, those who emphasise direct funding, and of course those who mix both methods. What then, is the implication? In a hierarchal model there are many junctions in which one can attack, the bodies involved as well as the money as it is being transferred. In the direct funding model there are only two junctions which can be attacked: the donor and the money on its way to the receiver.

Let us now focus on direct funding and how it is carried out. A number of weeks ago, a book dealing with jihad via hijra written by Abu Said al-Britani (an ISIS militant from the UK, currently in Syria) was published. Abu Said opens a window into jihad via money (jihad bil-mal), including direct funding: The preferred option is to transfer the money to the Islamic State, the Dawla. If you know a "brother" in the Islamic State – send the money directly to him. If you know a "brother", but the authorities are monitoring you, it is prudent to use a third party to transfer the money. If you do not know a "brother" in the Dawla, I will provide details how and where to send the money. You can also send money with a foreign fighter, to be used when he arrives in the Dawla (we see this in the different blogs). You can also decide not to send money to the Dawla, but rather use it in your home country, to help a foreign fighter in expenses required to travel to the Dawla or to help fund the family of a foreign fighter who has travelled to carry out jihad in the Islamic State.

Let us return to the option that you do not know a brother in the Islamic State and need instructions on how and where to transfer the money. In this case, the writer suggests using the KIK application in order to transfer the money to a contact in the capital cities via Western Union Bank.

All we have seen up until now has accumulated to the same spot—the cyber space: the funding sources, the transfer ways, and the world of the many connected to many phenomenon. Terror organisations make use of the cyber world to enlarge their fundraising, first of all by extensive and professional use of internet websites, forums and digital magazines. We see significant use of social networks in order to spread the message, networks like Twitter, Instagram, YouTube, Google+, FaceBook and Tumbler. From the moment the message is spread from many to many, the instructions regarding how to pay are transferred in the various applications. Telegram is the most used application, for it is considered to be more secure for the terrorists. The payment itself can be carried out via electronic means which are available in the cyber world, pre-paid cards and digital coins. In Twitter, instructions were available on how to use a pre-paid card named Cashu. There were also examples of the secure use of the Telegram application. In an online magazine, ISIS' Dabiq issue 11, theorganisation provides instructions on where to reach out in Telegram, in order to receive information regarding transfer of ransom money in return for two captives the organisation is holding.

After we see the innovations in the realm of terror fundraising, let us now see how it is reflected in the richest terror organisation today, ISIS. Independent funding starts in the territory in the group's control and continues outward. ISIS funds itself, amongst other ways, via criminal activity, kidnappings for ransom, extortion of farmers, stealing, trafficking human organs, trafficking women and so forth. It collects taxes from the population in the territory under its control, which serve a significant part of the organisation's income. The organisation also collects donations from the local population, although it is difficult to differentiate between donations and taxes. ISIS also utilises the natural resources in the territory under its control; mostly (but not only) oil and gas. It makes use of phosphate, cement, hydroelectric power plants, thermal power plans as well as antiquities and cultural elements. There are also one-time sources which usher in large amounts of money, such as cash held in banks in the areas which the organisation seized control of and various other assets. The organisation makes use of these incomes not only for its activity, but also to provide the population with public goods, an expenditure which only a hybrid organisation has. ISIS' independent funding is the most significant element in the funding of its activities, and according to various estimations sums up to a billion dollars a year.

ISIS' funding based on donations from outside its territory is not significant compared to its general income, but for organisations that are not hybrid, it could serve as a significant source of income. The fundraisers can send the money according to the traditional ways, to one of the organisation's finance centres, or to other places. It could be transferred directly to support foreign fighters, or for travel expenses, or to support their families or they may even take the money with them to the theatre of jihad. The donators can do this directly or via facilitators.

It is important to remember, that the wages paid to the activists are a significant portion of the organisation's expenses, and that foreign fighters receive a higher salary as compared to local fighters. Donors also transfer money to cells operating outside of the territory in ISIS' control. The money comes from various sources, including taking of loans, taking advantage of welfare policy in Western states and even theft. It must be noted that terror attacks are not necessarily expensive, and at times self-funding or just a small amount of help will be sufficient.

I have tried to present in this paper, the new characteristics that have to do with terror funding. In some organisations, these characteristics are stronger than in others. However, those that deal with preventing terror fundraising should wake up at an early stage and do what is needed, before it is too late. I would like to argue that the domain of countering traditional terror-fundraising is more successful than other areas of combating terror, mainly due to the cooperation at all levels (international, national and intra-national) and due to the involvement of civilian bodies in the fight.

Today, in addition to the security forces, we are aided by financial civilian bodies at all levels in order to prevent terror-fundraising, bodies which are subject to regulations or have a significant economic interest to cooperate. Starting with the FATF which is an international body, as well as bodies which provide financial services such as banks, lawyers' officers, accountants, etc. I argue that we must apply the same conditions to bodies in the cyber and technological worlds. Beginning with the establishment of a new body similar to the FATF which will be built by the G-7 or CTED on the international level, and continuing on to technological bodies which provide internet services, social networks and communication applications which are used to fund terror.

15

The Caliphate, Al-Qaeda and Global Jihad

Daniel Pipes

A question often asked is, 'What do the jihadis (Mujahideen) want'? The answer is surprisingly obscure as most of their attacks do not include clear demands. The horrific attacks on Mumbai in November 2008 and in Paris in November 2015 were carried out by suicide squads, with gunmen carrying out mass shootings. Elsewhere, they have resorted to machine gun assaults, beheadings, bombings, hijackings et al. After the attackers have been neutralised by the security forces, an assessment is carried out of the damage they caused and detectives attempt to trace the identities of the perpetrators, to look into possible motives. Shadowy websites then make post-hoc unauthenticated claims, which still belie the question, 'What do the jihadis want'?

Why do the motives go unexplained? Post the attacks on the United States on 11 September 2001, analysts are still speculating on the likely motives. In broad terms however, we can state that there are two general categories or motives for attacks. The first is to change specific policies of the state which has been targeted. As an example, this could pertain to seeking withdrawal of foreign troops from Iraq and Afghanistan or to get Riyadh to expel foreign troops from its soil. It could also be aimed at pressurising governments to end support for Israel or to pressurise New Delhi to cede control over Kashmir.

The second category is more broad based and is aimed at weakening non-Muslims in general, undermining their economy, creating fear in the minds of their populace and attempting to establish Muslim superiority. But both the categories point to something even larger. The jihadis seek to establish a world dominated by Muslims, Islam, Shari'a and the caliphate.

We see jihad take two forms, based on the relative strength of the Muslim population in an area. Where non-Muslims rule, the attempt is to gain control over the levers of power, and to be in charge. The aim is to overthrow kafir rule. There is no direct attempt to convert, but the war is a war for territory. Where Muslims rule, the aim is to apply Shari'a in its entirety. The hope or end state is for a pious, just, ruler who can make Muslims strong and rich and who can end their divisions. The end state of both is however a global caliphate. The Caliph rules over all the peoples of the world and implements Shari'a law in its entirety.

Brief History

The succession to Muhammad saw deep divisions in Islam which remains to this day. At the heart of the dispute was who would occupy the Prophets place at the head of the Muslim community, which even now creates a divide amongst Shias and Sunnis. The successors to Muhammad, however, oversaw the great Islamic conquests for the next three hundred years. The executive caliphate ended in 940s and though the title passed on, it was nominal. The last Abbasid caliphate in Baghdad ended in 1258 CE, following the Mongol sack of Baghdad. During the latter half of the Abbasid rule, Muslim rulers had however started using other titles, such as Sultan. Atatürk ended the caliphate on 3 March 1924, but the idea lived on as seen in the Khilafat movement from 1919-26.

The more recent articulations of a caliphate have been of Osama bin Laden, who wanted a "pious caliphate [that] will start from Afghanistan". His successor, Ayman al-Zawahiri, envisioned a caliphate through which, "history would make a new turn." As per Fazlur Rehman Khalil, another al-Qaeda leader: "Due to the blessings of jihad, America's countdown has begun. It will declare defeat soon," and will be followed by a caliphate. In 2005, al-Qaeda started the Sawt al-Khalifa radio station.

The Caliphate

Pronouncements by certain leaders and a general feeling amongst the population gave a sense that a caliphate was in the offing. At a Hizb ut-Tahrir meeting in Copenhagen, its imam, Muziz Abdullah, surveyed a hall filled to standing-room only capacity. "Ten years ago, when I started, it was totally unrealistic to think there could be a caliphate", he stated. "But now, people believe it could happen in a few years." Fatih Alev, an imam in Copenhagen, stated: "As of now, the caliphate is totally irrelevant. As of tomorrow, it could be relevant. I would not exclude it."

There was a sense of imminence of a caliphate amongst the common people too. As per Kerem Acar, a tailor in central Istanbul: "I won't live to see it, and my children won't, but one day maybe my children's children will see someone declare himself the caliph, like the pope, and have an impact." Ertuğul Orel, a cafe owner in Istanbul, expressed a hope for the caliphate, but did not believe it would come about. "A caliphate means, there would be [only] one voice", he said. "But I know, neither the Americans nor the Europeans will ever allow it." Ali Bulaç, a Turkish authority on Islam and Turkey was quite explicit when he stated, "The concept of the caliphate is very much alive in the collective memory of society".

Much the same view was expressed by Zeyno Baran, an expert on Hizb ut-Tahrir. "A few years ago people laughed at [it]. But now that bin Laden, Zarqawi, & [others] are saying they want to recreate the caliphate, people are taking them seriously." Posters with big, bright-red lettering calling for the establishment of an Islamic Caliphate in Lebanon can now be seen around many streets in Sidon, pasted up by members of Hizb ut-Tahrir. The posters call for "reviving an Islamic Caliphate state after the enemies in the malicious and colonial West underestimated our spiritual force. We will only come out strong with an Islamic state'."

As per James Brandon in the CSM: "Hizb ut-Tahrir promises that a revived caliphate will end corruption and bring prosperity.... It will let Muslims challenge, and ultimately conquer, the West." He quotes Abdullah Shakr, a Jordanian member of the group: "The Muslim world has resources like oil but it lacks the leadership that will rule us by Islamic law and make this jihad that the whole world is afraid of." Shakr indicates that the caliphate's success will bring more conversions to Islam and turn the whole world Muslim. However, the route to the Caliphate, as propagated by Hizb ut-Tahrir is gradual and mostly peaceful. For the al-Qaeda, it is violent and revolutionary.

Beyond the Muslim world, the understanding was of a different order. In 2004, Dick Cheney when talking about Osama bin Laden, explicitly stated that "they talk about wanting to re-establish what you could refer to as the seventh-century caliphate," to be "governed by Sharia law, the most rigid interpretation of the Koran", he said. Many others in the George W. Bush administration followed suit and in 2005, The Daily Telegraph, rang the warning bells, stating, "Fanatics around the world dream of the Caliph's return"

The idea did seem impossible at that time and the Bush-hating Left, including Islam specialists (Kenneth M. Pollack, John L. Esposito, Shibley Telhami) pooh-poohed the whole topic. Investigative journalist Robert Dreyfuss, on the aspiration to a caliphate was rather dismissive of the idea. He described as 'idiotic' the notion that Islamist forces wished to establish a caliphate from North Africa to Southeast Asia. "This was utter nonsense", he said. "What was happening was that those in the administration who made such declarations based them on what they read on al-Qaeda and other jihadi websites". "Such threats", he added, "were in the nature of fantasies and should be treated as such."

When a Caliphate suddenly appeared on June 29, 2014, announced by "Islamic State" and headed by Caliph Ibrahim, it was unanticipated. The announcement was followed by spectacular military victories, especially Mosul, which gave it unique global prestige. Groups such as Boko Haram paid it homage and it had an electrifying effect on Sunni Muslims. The potential impact of the Islamic state as a Caliphate is that it boosts the dream of a single rule across 'Islamdom' and beyond, inspires others to do the same and radicalises Islamist movements.

16

Terrorism: An Alternate Perspective

Ajai Sahni

It is an extremely interesting concept to imagine the world as a live grenade. However, the explosive content in that grenade is not terrorism, but a whole range of other problems that the world is confronted with—demography, the human abuse of the environment, the unnatural and excessive burden we have placed on earth etc., but certainly not terrorism. In this presentation, I attempt to outline a set of alternate viewpoints with regard to commonly held beliefs about terrorism.

Some analysts believe that financial and communication networks are the life blood of terrorism, but that is not so. The lifeblood of terrorism is terror. It is the armed strength of terrorist groups and the will to use it for limitless violence to achieve political goals. If the armed strength of terrorist groups is destroyed, there is little that they can do, regardless of the strength of their financial and communication networks. Financial networks and communication technologies like Twitter, Facebook, et al., are not terrorist technologies, any more than a car is a terrorist technology because it is used as a car bomb, or a horse carriage was a terrorist technology when it was used as the first vehicle-borne IED (improvised explosive device) in New York in 1920.

There is also a belief that terrorism is one of the most difficult phenomena to understand. I would like to suggest that terrorism is, in fact, one of the most frequently *intentionally* misunderstood phenomena in the world. Nation states, groups and individuals choose to interpret terrorism differently in different circumstances. They do so because it is to their advantage. Consequently, vast areas of the world have been destabilised. Environments have been created wherein groups have been resourced and armed. Over time, these groups transform and reinvent themselves, and strike back at the very powers and entities that created them. When the blowback comes, the refrain changes and the world is told 'we are in a global war'.

It is important to understand how narratives are shaped. To equate terrorism as it exists today with global war belies an understanding of what global war is. A simple calculation of how many people have died due to terrorist attacks and how many were killed in the great wars—World War I and World War II—would be sufficient to counter any such comparison. We are seeing the late 20th and early 21st Centuries as among the most peaceful times for mankind in history. Why then are we talking of global networks at this time? Is the narrative being shaped in a particular way in order to achieve a specific objective?

By the early 2000s, more than 30,000 people had been killed in Jammu and Kashmir alone.[3] Yet no one spoke of global war. When 320 people were killed by armed Islamic groups, mostly Ingush and Chechen, in September 2004 in Beslan, North Ossetia (an autonomous republic in the North Caucasus region of the Russian Federation) of whom 187 were children, there was little talk of the world being at war. Yet, when 12 people were killed in Paris, in the attack on *Charlie Hebdo*—a French satirical magazine, in January 2015, the world was aghast. Why? At about the time the attack on Charlie Hebdo took place, some 2000 people were slaughtered by the Boko Haram in three days of mindless violence in Baga, Nigeria. That did not agitate the conscience of the world, but the killing of a dozen Frenchmen in the attack on Charlie Hebdo did. Why? Are we being manipulated? Are the interests of certain states pushing this agenda? And are these the same states that have created the crisis in the first place?

The Western powers entered Syria and Iraq ostensibly to promote democracy and remove what was perceived to be brutal dictatorships, they created a conflict, which is still ongoing, and has brought death to hundreds of thousands of people in that region. That is considered virtuous because democracy was being promoted! After years of conflict, the establishment of democracy in the region remains a far cry, which begs the question as to why the states were destabilised in the first place. More importantly, when the Russian forces moved into the region, the narrative that was propagated was that the entry of Russian forces was destabilising the world order! Why was the Russian intervention considered as destabilising, when intervention by the Western powers was not?

Let us now consider networks. What is the power of the ISIS? What has the ISIS done which has not been done by many terrorist groups earlier? Have the terrorists groups not beheaded anyone before? I watched a video in the year 2006 of a 9-year old boy slitting the throat of a prisoner in Swat, Pakistan. The ISIS was not there at that time. What the ISIS has done and is currently doing in terms of brutal killings, has been done by many organisations in earlier times. The difference today is that the ISIS has fused its brutality with great mastery and sophistication in the communication technologies that are available today. By creating a sense of shock, it has exaggerated both its military victories and its own brutalities. It understands the psychological impact of its actions on the public. Though it has killed a very small number of people compared to the vast slaughters that are ongoing in West Asia today, the impact of those killings has been magnified many times. It is not terrorism that constitutes the greatest danger to the people of the region or the world.

Today, the ISIS has got money because certain assets have gone over to it. Its members carry out extortion, because, if you have a gun and you are willing to use it, the money will come. As I stated earlier, the life blood of terrorism is terror. You can document how the money comes, how it is transferred, who are the resources, whether it is extortion or whether it is believers or non-believers. But the money is coming only because of the power of the gun and the willingness of the terrorist to use it. Through the gun, money, support by the populace, and support by certain states which have a stake in terrorism, will be forthcoming. State interests are created due to rivalries that exist in societies such as between the Shia and the Sunni, or due to separatist tendencies such as that of the Tamils in Sri Lanka or the Sikhs in Punjab, etc. But where are all the real resources, the weapons, coming from? The ISIS does not manufacture weapons, so where do the weapons in the possession of ISIS come from?

What is a network? Somebody slits someone's throat and hacks someone to death in a London street or a couple of Pakistani origin people go to America and shoot up 14 people and the refrain heard is that the 'ISIS has come'. Why? Just because a group of people have pledged themselves to the ISIS? Was there a transfer of resources? Was there a transfer of capability, the transfer of weaponry? Was there an enhancement of their own natural capabilities?

Let us say a group is inspired by Mao and starts a Maoist rebellion. The group goes out and commits atrocities and executes people in the name of Mao. Is that justifiable grounds to state that there is a network between China and India? Obviously, the answer is in the negative. There is no network, the group simply draws inspiration from the Maoist ideology. Groups learn from methods everywhere, not just from the example of the Islamic State. Yes, the ISIS has put out books and manuals, but the Maoists do it too. There are manuals available for all sorts of violent activities all over. The point is, who is using them, where are they using them, and are they coming together?

When we talk about networks, we need to understand the local dynamic. If we defeat the local dynamic, the global network disappears. Once the LTTE was destroyed in Sri Lanka, all its sympathisers over the world could do precious little to once again instigate violence in the state. There could be other problems related to political and constitutional issues, resentments over long-held grievances and cultural antipathies, but there will be no terrorism. If terrorism is defeated locally, the networks will disappear.

What is the essence of the dynamic that defines cooperation and rivalry among terrorist formations? It is identical to the essence of cooperation, collaboration and adversary relationships in any other organisation. Robert Michels once spoke of the 'iron law of oligarchy', that whatever the purpose of an institution, once the power structure has come into being, it will do whatever is necessary to preserve and augment its own power, even if it is engaged in activities that are diametrically opposed to its original intent. And this is the essence also of cooperation and collaboration between terror groups.

We hear of the ISIS coming to Pakistan and India, simply because some people are waving the ISIS flag. What needs consideration however is, have the capacities and capabilities of local formations been altered by the coming of the ISIS? Who are the groups who are joining them? Two categories of groups join the ISIS in different parts of the world: The first category is one that is not threatened by the ISIS in terms of their local dominance. They are already powerful groups, and feel that they will get more attention by saying 'we are ISIS' at this juncture, because ISIS is the big thing. These same groups were saying we are al-Qaeda just a few years back, because at that point of time, every fire cracker that went off was al-Qaeda. So that's one category that joins them.

The second category is that of the weak groups—groups that have no identity of their own, groups that are under tremendous pressure, like segments of the Indian Mujahideen or those remnant groupings in Bangladesh which have been hacking people to death since several years, but are now jumping onto the ISIS bandwagon in order to get free publicity. It suits the interests of the ISIS to say these groups are theirs, because it magnifies the image of the ISIS. But looking at the situation more realistically, we find that neither has the threat level in Bangladesh been altered nor have the capacities of the terror groups been augmented. There is also no change in command and control structures. These are the elements that define whether there is a network or not.

We have certain categories and certain groups which have simply and opportunistically shifted allegiance to the ISIS. The Boko Haram and segments of al-Shabab have shifted their allegiance to the ISIS, largely due to internal differences. We see the same happening in parts of Afghanistan with the Taliban, where certain segments have broken away and now claim to be ISIS. In inter-factional clashes, they kill each other and also kill civilians. Civilian killings occur when there are rivalries, with each group killing civilians competitively, leading to an escalation in civilian deaths and also to an escalation in terrorist fatalities. There is a documented fratricidal contest between these groups in multiple theatres today. And these rivalries follow the same dynamic, the same logic of consolidation of power; of certain sections, of certain groups or subgroups which have secured dominance either in a certain area or within a certain population.

There is a third category too—the lone wolves. We must be cautious here as lone wolves are never alone. They have always fed from ideas that they have borrowed from other groups. They have learnt from others in terms of example, or technology, or method. And we must also understand that they are also a part of a coordinated campaign which has been very consciously thought out by the Islamist terrorist organisations, which have been supported by the very states that are now victims of this violence.

The idea of a leaderless Jihad was proposed years ago, after 9/11 though, by the al-Qaeda theorists. We now have the idea of the "management of savagery". The intention is to create a condition of what is described as 'savagery' by the theoreticians, where they seek the collapse of the state, internally, and then in the situation of that collapse, with no alternatives available for governance, for supply of public goods and civil security, they feel that this is the opportunity within which the *jihadi* forces will be able to establish their dominance.

But they have not secured the collapse of any single state in the world on their own. That collapse has been presented to them by the intervention of other states. The ISIS did not cause the collapse of the Syrian state, nor did the al-Qaeda cause the collapse of the Iraqi state. The external powers did that. In the last decade and a half since 2001, since 9/11, it is the western world, the so called civilised world, which has compromised every value of democracy and every pretension of human rights that it resorts to impose on others, which has led to the collapse of states.

In conclusion, the power of the terrorist groups is being exaggerated. This exaggeration, this production of paranoia has very specific domestic, political and global strategic goals. There is a tremendous rise of the extreme right wing in certain countries, and they are the ones which continue to propagate this belief. The Islamist terrorist related fatalities in India have come down from about 4500 in 2001 to 173 fatalities in 2015. We need to question whether Islamic terrorism is the biggest threat to India or does the threat lie elsewhere? We have not had any serious Islamist terrorist activities in India for some time, apart from the occasional incidents from Jammu & Kashmir.

There are networks, as their inevitably will be. There are networks today because the world is networked and not because the terrorists are brilliant originators of new technologies. The terrorists use the technologies that are openly available and the state must develop the capacities to counter these technologies, preferably before these technologies are applied to destructive use. We are always chasing the tail of the tiger, because we refuse to set a trap. The way to fight the tiger is to prepare, to set a trap; we must be ready to shoot the tiger before he comes. In a similar manner, we do not have to wait for terrorists to jump over the wall into the Pathankot Air Force compound before initiating a response. Such groups must be eliminated well before they reach the intended target.

There is a problem in our orientation and this problem is intentionally created by states which will not allow clarity to be brought to the issue of terrorism because it suits them. Every state has a stake in terrorism in some way or the other. And that is why they do not want non-discriminatory action against terrorists. That is why this nonsense of one man's terrorist being another man's freedom fighter has been given currency. This argument is puerile; people have multiple identities. A terrorist can also be a freedom fighter. A person is a terrorist because of the methods used. The same person could be a freedom fighter if his objective is freedom. And yet this infantile argument will be heard in every learned discussion in the world, at every learned forum. Why? Because they want to paralyse a coordinated response against all terrorists in the world. And 'they' are some of the most powerful nations of the world.

17

An Inside View

Baker Atyani

In my view, terrorism stands today as one of the worlds biggest and perhaps the least comprehended phenomena. Militant groups are classified as terror groups on broad lines which is where we fail to sometimes handle the problem. Such groups indeed terrorise, just as some states commit heinous acts of terror against civilians in pursuit of its goals. My 18 years of work in conflict zones, studying violent extremist groups, have made me believe that the more subjective terminology they fall under is Militant groups. In this article, I thus will not use the term 'terrorist groups', but will instead use the term 'militant groups', because the former has become more of a political term that is been used loosely recently by some for convenience of purpose.

Militant groups in my observation exhibit the same social patterns and behaviour as a general human society, with their own set of acceptable norms, identified enemies, insecurities, professional rivalries, competition, and forged alliances against common threat. Each militant group is born out of different reasons; some on religious grounds some on political demands and others in ethnic and sectarian shades. I have interviewed the leaders and members of main militant groups such as Osama bin Laden, Ayman al-Zawahiri in Afghanistan, Abdulmalik Rigi, the leader of Iranian militant group Jundullah in no mans triangle between Iran, Pakistan and Afghanistan, Abu Bakr Ba'ashir, the spiritual leader of Jama'a Islamia (JI) in Indonesia, Salamat Hashim, the founder of Moro Islamic Liberation Front (MILF) in Southern Philippines and later his successor Haji Murad Ibrahim, including the echelons of Taliban in Afghanistan and Pakistan. Every group has its own argument for carrying guns and resorting to violence instead of peaceful means to attain its objectives. They are similar on certain grounds, but sometimes quite different in approach.

The drive to unveil militancy and understand this different mindset and ideology led me to the jungles of Solo Island in Southern Philippines in mid 2012, to interview one of the main Abu Sayyaf Group leaders which went wrong as would happen in any corrupt society and I was held hostage for 18 months! I lived as a hostage and shared their life and their fears, and had the occasion to observe first hand, how they are manipulated, driven close by wrong strategies and divided by playing on human factors like greed, competition and fear.

After the death of its founder Abdulrazzaq Janjalani in 1998, the Islamic Movement better knows as Abu Sayyaf Group (ASG), turned into more of a cluster of communities run by one strong family that provided food and weapons to smaller, poorer families and individuals. In Solo Island alone, there are 8-10 communities, all called ASG; every community has a leader who is responsible for their food and protection even from other ASG communities. This leader is in touch with the main leader of ASG, Radolan Sahiron, who belongs to one of the most influential families in Solo.

In my case, Kasman Sawadjan who leads a community of 2 families planned my kidnapping; he cooperated and coordinated with the following:

- Individuals who did not belong to the group but wanted to benefit from the exercise. In my case, I was tipped off by a journalist who provided information to the group. The group usually adopts this approach of utilising external resources when it lacks tentacles in cities and outside the jungle. The resource is usually either a believer or a beneficiary.
- Corrupt elements in law enforcement agencies, who acted as

negotiators, but were continuously in touch over cell phone with the kidnappers.

- The community of civilians in the jungle that tips off such groups, inadvertently providing cover and protection. These civilians are always aware of the hostages' places and militant hideouts. They are either family members, supporters, beneficiaries, or at times people simply coerced to obey the groups' traditions. Denying can get them pushed out of the area or even killed.
- The smaller and poorer families who joined the Militants community of Sawadjan, offering logistic support in an attempt to get a piece of the pie. This community became 8 families after my kidnapping.
- The main leader of ASG, Rodolan Sahiron who was not initially part of the kidnapping, also got involved to get his standard 20 percent share out of any income in exchange for letting the groups use ASG name (20 percent is the said share in Islam for the Supreme Leader from the spoils of war also called "Ghana'em").

This was the perfect example of crime evolving into militancy using the name of jihad. Catching a potentially lucrative target not only forged cooperation between various armed groups but also stirred competition between two key ASG leaders, Radolan Sahiron and Kasman Sawadjan. Because of this struggle for bounty, I was relocated 11 times during these 18 months. During this period, many a times were machetes put at my throat, and I was threatened with beheading if ransom was not paid.

The rivalry in this case was not ideological, but based on personal interest and on claiming the legitimacy—as we can see in the case of Baghdadi and Zawahiri and between Taliban leader Mullah Akhtar Mansour and Mulla Mohamad Rasool Akhond. Any military effort for my release, or any external threat would diminish these differences and bring the groups together to protect their ground and guard their bounty.

During my 18 months in ASG's custody, three communities, not only cooperated in logistics, but also in attacks against the Philippine

Marines. One such attack was based on a request made by an ASG group in Basilan Island, where they were facing a massive military operation. The idea was to engage the Philippine Marines in another front to reduce pressure in Basilan front. The second was when the main base of ASG came under attack by the Philippine Marines. ASG then joined hands to counter the operation, and they were rewarded by the main ASG leader Radolan Sahiron by sending them boxes of ammunition after they came to his community's rescue. One month before this attack, Sawadjan was preparing for an encounter in case Sahiron attacks his community., thus proving that external threats usually unite militant groups.

We saw the same pattern in Afghanistan after 9/11. Here, different militant groups such as Libyan Islamic fighting group and the Attawhid wa'l Jihad group of Abu Mu'saab al-Zarqawi were not part of al-Qaeda. But when the world dealt with militant groups in Afghanistan as one problem, these groups started cooperating against the common enemy and later merged into al-Qaeda, leading not only to expansion in the size of the militant outfit, but fortifying its strength, bringing more ground under its hold.

Cooperation no doubt makes them live long and fight better turning them more lethal. Groups with more links and connections tend to survive longer. According to some studies, al-Qaeda has between 25-30 connections with militants groups around the world. ISIS is growing even bigger with its external connections. Rivalry might not necessarily weaken the militant groups; in fact this could push them to be more innovative to win and dominate. The recent attack on Radisson Blu hotel in Bamako, Mali was a result of the al-Qaeda-ISIS struggle for dominance in the wake of Paris attacks. Also, the new al-Qaeda branch for Indian sub continent announced in 2015, can be seen as part of this competition between al-Qaeda and ISIS.

My observation of these militant groups shows that when state actors—mainly intelligence agencies—sponsor one group to counter the other, or to use against another country, it leads to a mushroom of militant groups coming out from the womb of the sponsored group. This can be seen in Syria very clearly.

Proxy wars do not easily extinguish themselves. "Ugly stability" with one side victorious, is usually the solution if a proxy war is launched. In case of Syria where militants want regime change, even if U.S. Saudis, Qataris, Turks, Iranians, and Russians agreed to forgo all future support for their respective factions in Syria, the war would not burn itself out overnight. It is too late! Successful strategies to counter violent extremist groups must begin by subjectively defining the violent group in any society, understand its goals and targets and deal with them based on that. Every militant group calls for a customised counter strategy. A broad-base solution will be ineffective if not harmful.

State classification of its endogenous problem as terrorism is not enough to judge the issue on terrorism grounds. It might often be a reaction to political or economic suppression especially in countries with weak democracies and poor human rights record. According to a recent survey, the University of Maryland found that militants in Syria were motivated primarily by revenge and regime change, not by religion or larger regional issues. The Government of the Philippines and the MILF identified the problem of Mindanao correctly as political. This subsequently led to the Comprehensive Agreement on the Bangsamoro. The Irish Republic Army (IRA) and the British Government reached the same peace agreement after years of fighting.

In conclusion, I would say unless countries and state enterprises stop using armed groups as proxies, improve human rights conditions, strengthen institutions, fight corruption and uphold rule of law, the world will keep witnessing hotspots, conflict zones, and political groups go violent.

18

Religion, Ideology and Jihad

Lt Gen K.T. Parnaik

Religion remains a binding force for communities. It compels the society to build faith, provides emotional support and creates hope. The 'known-unknown' has permeated into our lives as the sole constant—one that shows us the path of righteousness, teaches tolerance and defines parameters of societal living. It provides solace, kindles hope and in a sublime manner, motivates human beings to act. Religious scriptures and their interpretations by the clerics, historians and ideologues, hold sway over our behaviour and that is where religion becomes the single most important politico-ideological default mechanism, for achieving one's goals. When used to propagate violence, it is more lethal and intractable than its secular part. It comes as no surprise then, that the motives of the terrorists of 9/11 infamy, as revealed by the instructions that guided their final days, were intensely and profoundly religious.

Primordial fear has long been recognised as a tool for dissuasion, subjugation, punishment and force compliance. The current wave of global terrorism perpetuated by extreme groups like Daesh (IS or ISIS), al-Qaeda, Boko Haram and al Shabab has become a scourge to the human race. Their nihilistic vision and their genocidal agenda is aimed at establishing a pan Islamic Caliphate, enforcing Sharia and subjugating/converting the non-believers in the name of Allah. The format is reminiscent of the Great Ottoman Empire.

Religious violence as a tool for achieving political goals has an ancient history. In the First Century CE, the Sicarii, a splinter group of the Jewish Zealots, opposed the Roman occupation of Judea and attempted to expel them and their sympathisers from the area. They carried small daggers (called sicae), concealed in their cloaks, and in public gatherings, pulled them out to attack Romans and Hebrew Roman sympathisers alike, blending into the crowd after the deed to escape detection. Similarities can be seen in the aims and methodologies of the ancient Sicarii and the modern day terrorist. In the 11th Century, the Hashashin (a name given to the medieval Nizari Ismailis and which translates as assassins) emerged from a split within Ismailism—itself a branch of Shia Islam. The Hashashin posed a military threat to Sunni Seljuq authority within their territories by capturing and inhabiting many unconnected mountain fortresses throughout Persia, and later Syria, under the leadership of Hassan-i Sabbah. Feudal Japan had the Ninjas—whose functions included espionage, sabotage, infiltration, assassination and guerrilla warfare. Their covert methods of waging irregular warfare were deemed "dishonourable" and "beneath" the Samurai-caste, who observed strict rules about honour and combat.

Historical Construct

The Arab conquest unleashed in the 7th Century was seen as a form of jihad against the Christian Crusaders. Some historians argue that the likely cause was hunger and desertification of the Arabian Peninsula. Many however, are inclined to the belief that the causative factors were religious.

Most Islamic theologians, in the period 750-1250 CE, understood jihad as a military endeavour. When conquest stagnated, the Caliphate broke up into smaller states. Permanent jihad became unfeasible and was postponed from historic to messianic times. However, exceptions like the massacres by Timurlane (14th Century), Bader Khan (1840), Hamidian massacres (1890) and the Arminian genocide (1915-21) were all religiously motivated and the jihad-terror construct was established as a form of religious duty. The Koranic interpretations of jihad is an idiomatic expression, which means "striving in the name of God" (al-Jihad–fi-Sabil-Allah). Within the context of classical Islamic law it refers to struggle against those who don't believe in God while some talk of the inner spiritual struggle or outer physical struggle against enemies of Islam. In Twelver Shia Islam, jihad is one of the ten pillars of the religion. It appears in 164 verses in Quran and 199 times in standard collection of Hadith Bukhari.

The despair of Muslims at the fall of the Ottoman Empire, the only symbol of Islamic power after World War I, shattered their cohesion. Worse still, their lands lay under occupation of the European powers. Once oil was discovered in the Arabian peninsula, the West descended on their homelands, strengthening their hold on the energy resource and installing proxy governments. The Muslim world was divided as the richer nations turned a blind eye to the poorer ones. Subjugation in their own backyard was the ultimate humiliation. Anarchism, in league with rising nationalism, became the most prominent Ideology post 19th Century. Revolutionary nationalism continued to motivate political violence against the colonial masters in the 20th Century. Largely successful anti-colonial campaigns after WW II, saw the rise of independence movements.

Not all Muslims adapted to western industrialisation, modernisation and secular democratic system, which was perceived as violation of Islamic faith and beliefs. Islamist vision, framed on purely religious dogmas, rejected even the legitimacy of their own governments in the Arabic world. Overthrowing these governments became an Islamic agenda. A mournful lament "Islam in danger" morphed into a rallying point—a powerful war cry. The clarion call finally led to the Colour Revolutions that unfolded in the Middle East and Magreb.

Ideological Impact

The roots of Islamic Ideology in the sub-continent can be traced to the Deobandi School (JeI and Jamaat-e-Ulema) pioneered by Syed Abul A'la Maududi. In the Middle East, Wahhabism was propelled by Ahle-Hadith and Ikwan-ul-Musalmeen or the Muslim Brotherhood under Hasan-Al-Bana. The Islamic ideological ferment for state formation in the sub-continent (1700-1947) is based on Global Ummah, the Hakumat-e-Ilahi or sovereignty of God, as opposed to sovereignty of nation state, or the Fiqh. The Indian Muslims dismissed Gandhi's vision of modern secular state as incompatible with Islam, which finally led to the formation of Pakistan as the first contemporary Islamic state. Paradoxically, Pakistan's disintegration reinforced the view amongst many Muslims, that Islam was the only basis for integration of an ethnically diverse nation. But the centre of power and public institutions that supported the idea of Pakistan as a theocratic state, merely turned it into a haven for terrorist groups that used jihad as a means to extend Islamic space. The tremor spread to Afghanistan and today the Af-Pak region has become the epicentre of global terrorism.

Daesh (IS or ISIS) is yet another manifestation of Sunni theocratic revivalism. The ideological impetus comes from 18th century theologist, Mahummad-bin-Abdal-Wahhab of Najd (Saudi Arabia), who offered a vision of the Caliphate, reborn with leaders who can cleanse it of impure practices and heresies such as 'Shiism'. Their thirst for purity is thirst for blood. Daesh is an advocate of Dar-el-Harb (House of War) and its vision is to target the 'far enemy', the 'near enemy' and countries that have occupied Islamic territories.

Modern Muslim clerics and historians have severely criticised the interpretations of Koranic teachings, adapted by the Wahhabi/Salafi cult and have termed this holy war as a 'maverick jihadism', as they consider their acts to be egregious violations of the Islamic laws. The fundamentalist organisations perceive ideology as the 'centre of gravity' and gravitate towards a collection of violent Islamic thoughts called 'Qutbism'. The tenets of Qutbism being:

- Belief that Muslims have deviated from true Islam and must return to pure Islam as practised during the time of Muhammed.
- Path to pure Islam is through literal and strict interpretation of Quran and Hadith along with implementation of Muhammed's command.
- Muslims must interpret original sources individually without following the interpretations of the Islamic scholars.
- Any interpretation of Quran from historical contextual perspective is a corruption and that majority of Islamic history and classical jurisprudential tradition is mere sophistry.

In response, Islamic teachers and historians state that neither Osama bin Laden nor Ayman-al Zawahiri were graduates of Islamic universities and their proclamations ignore fourteen centuries of Muslim scholarship, taking form of anti-US grievances and Quranic quotations referring to early Muslim wars against the Arab idolaters. They also question the religious credentials of Islamist theorist or Qutbist's. Except Syed Abul A'la Maududi and Abdullah Yusuf Azzam, none of Qutbism's main theoreticians trained at Islam recognised centres of learning. Hassan-al-Bana was a teacher and community activist, Muhammed-Abd-al-Salam-Faraz was an electrician, Ayaman-al-Zawahiri a physician, and Osama bin Laden was a businessman. Ali-Goma, former Grand Mufti of Egypt stated that not only for Islam but in general, 'terrorism', cannot be born of religion. It is a product of corrupt minds, hardened hearts and arrogant egos—and corruption, destruction and arrogance are not known to the Divine.

The above notwithstanding, Daesh, Boko Haram, al-Qaeda, al Shabab, Taliban, Sipah-e-Saheba, and Lashkar-e-Janghvi, all follow the intolerant Wahhabi/Salafi ideology. Non-Muslims, Sufis and Shias are targeted by Wahhabi, Deobandi and Jaamatis in the same way as the socialist and leftist proletarians were assaulted by Mussolini bandits, Jews by Nazi's and the bourgeoise Kulaks and Trotskyist by Stalin. We thus see a symbiotic relationship between religion, ideology and jihad. If ideology is the centre of gravity, which interprets religious teachings and Hadith's propagated by theologists, it generates religious edicts, dogmas or fatwas, which lead to jihad. Terror is the means to achieve the politico-ideological goal of the fundamentalist groups or so called Caliphs. The centrality of religion and framed theological pronouncements remain the key to the ideology adopted by the global terrorist. It is clear from the narrative that Islam as the central idea built on religious scriptures and teachings, has been idolised into a war cry by the theologist for whom 'terror' is the instrument to regain their lost glory. The jury is still out on whether the warped mind-set of groups such as Daesh and al-Qaeda can subjugate their target enemies, or would by their actions, devastate the Faith of the Faithful.

19

Religious and Theological Underpinnings of Global Islamist Terror

Sultan Shahin

The ease and swiftness with which the so-called Islamic State and the self-declared khilafat of Abu Bakr al-Baghdadi has attracted over 30,000 Muslims from 100 countries around the globe in just one year has surprised many. But this should not have come as a surprise to us in India. Muslim love for the idea of global Khilafat is well-known. From Indian subcontinent alone, less than a hundred years ago, at least 18,000 Muslims had left their homes, even government jobs and marched off to fight for the last Ottoman Khilafat. This was madness, pure and simple. Most ruined their lives and some died. But they are considered ghazis and martyrs. Important clerics including Maulana Abul Kalam Azad issued fatwas calling for Jihad or Hijrat (emigration) from British India, which was considered Darul Harb (Land of conflict, ruled by infidels), as a religious duty.

So, for a large section of Muslims the lure of a Khilafat that would rule the world, eliminate all other religions, particularly all forms of idolatry, establish the truth of Islam, is nothing new. When Baghdadi announced his khilafat, it was welcomed in many Muslim newspapers in India. An influential cleric from Nadwatul Ulama, went so far as to post a letter to the so-called Khalifa on his Facebook page, addressing him as Ameerul Momineen, spiritual leader of all Muslims. He faced no protest, not even from Nadwa or Darul uloom Deoband.

With the so-called Islamic State proudly broadcasting its monstrous brutalities and inhuman practices like sex slavery, the community is embarrassed and support is now muted. But this can only be described as hypocrisy. India's most popular Islamic preacher and Ahl-e-Hadithi televangelist Zakir Naik has been saying for years, that "Allah has made halal for Muslims sex with slaves and women captured in war." Muslim religious leaders have never protested. But when ISIS takes these fatwas and Wahhabi/Salafi teachings to their logical conclusion, actually kidnaps and makes Yazidi, Christian and Shia women sex slaves, the community is embarrassed and some clerics start saying Islam has nothing to do with terrorism.

Of course, Islam has nothing to do with terrorism. It is a spiritual path to salvation, not a political ideology for dominating the world. Prophet Mohammad (pbuh) was a mystic who was eventually appointed a messenger of God. There are innumerable verses in the Quran that call for peace at all costs, even going to the extent of saying that murder of one innocent person amounts to genocide of humanity and protection given to one innocent amounts to saving humanity (Quran 5:32). The same is also true of narrations of Prophet's supposed sayings, Ahadith (pl. of Hadith). Prophet's own conduct (Seerat) shows that he accepted peace even at the cost of justice and fairness for Muslims in the famous treaty of Hudaibiya. To avoid bloodshed in the Battle of the Trench (Ghazwah al-Khandaq, 627 CE), he secured the city of Medina behind a ditch he dug along with his companions around Medina. He declared a general Amnesty for all Meccans after conquering it without bloodshed (629 CE), when Meccans were apprehending a general massacre as was the prevailing custom of those times. So not only does Quran specifically forbid all violence against innocents and repeatedly warns against aggression, but the Prophet himself avoided violence as much as possible in the most trying times of Islam's infancy.

It is true that madrasas and mosques do not overtly preach

violence and terrorism. But it is also true that text books in madrasas do preach supremacism, xenophobia, exclusivism and intolerance. Thus they do the groundwork for militant ideologies by instilling in their students a binary thinking of Muslim/Kafir as opposites who cannot co-exist. As a result, some Muslims self-segregate and alienate themselves from the mainstream. A global Muslim missionary organisation Tablighi Jamaat, for instance, which has up to 150 million adherents in over 200 countries now, focuses entirely on segregating Muslims from the mainstream, asking them to maintain a separate identity, and prohibiting them from following any customs they may have in common with the non-Muslim majority. This Wahhabi/Salafi organisation was recently banned from university campuses in Pakistani Punjab but faces no such restriction in India.

Indeed, a Muslim is bombarded from all sides with sermons calling for jihad; a jihad, which is shorn of all its spiritual content and used simply as a synonym for qital, warfare. Even historical fiction written by 20th century Urdu novelist Nasim Hejazi, for instance, can be taken as a call for Jihad, far more effective than any overt Jihadi literature. In most popular Urdu fairy tales, Dāstān-e-Amīr Hamzah, for instance, the central character is fighting with demons who do not believe in oneness of God and are thus kafir. The devotional poetry a Muslim listens to at Sufi shrines contain lines like the following: "*Aaj bhi darte hain kafir Haidari Talwar se,*" meaning, even today the kafirs are afraid of the sword of Hazrat Ali, the fourth caliph. Even the first biographies of the Prophet, written by Arabs, called them "Maghazi Rasulullah," meaning battle accounts of the Prophet. The first Muslims, the Arabs, could not celebrate his devotion to peace, moderation, Huqooqul Ibad (human rights) and mystical approach to religion. They could only hail him as a hero presenting him as a great warrior which he was not. He barely lifted a sword once or twice, 14 years after prophethood, at the age of 54, purely in defence. The prayer a Muslim has been hearing week after week in every Friday sermon for 1400 years is for victory over kuffar (infidels), establishment of the true religion of Islam, dominance over the whole world, elimination of idolatry from the planet, and so on, all generating supremacism, exclusivism, xenophobia and intolerance.

The idea of a permanent confrontation with the kafir, thus, runs through our veins. In verses often quoted by militant ideologues, God assures Muslims in two places in Quran (8:12 and 3: 151) that "He will cast terror into the hearts of the Kuffars (Unbelievers)." This is a contextual verse, like some others, similarly militant and intolerant, revealed during the course of the existential wars waged by the Muslims in early Islam. Any rational Muslim would say today that these contextual war verses do not apply to us anymore. But you will not find even those moderate scholars seeking to refute terrorist ideologies saying that. In fact, the refutations go on to actually justify the core theology of terror and violence.

A hundred thousand copies of an Arabic book titled "Refuting ISIS" has recently been distributed in Syria and Iraq. It is also available online in English. The author Shaykh Muhammad Al-Yaqoubi is, of course, sincere in his refutation. But he too quotes from the same set of end-time prophesies, seeking to prove that Baghdadi and his clique are idiots and should be fought, thus giving credibility to these same series of millenarian prophesies. So what he actually ends up doing amounts to strengthening ISIS' propaganda of the allegedly coming apocalypse. Unlike al-Qaeda, which did not talk so much about apocalypse, ISIS vision is largely apocalyptic. They base the justification for their war as being the prophesied end-times war. They sacrificed many men capturing a militarily insignificant town called Dabiq (which is also the name of their mouthpiece) because the end-times prophecies refer to a war in this town.

Apocalyptic prophesies are one of the chief tools used by ISIS to attract Muslim youth to be part of an end-time war. If the world is going to end in a few years' time, with Islam conquering the world, as is prophesied, decimating all infidels, why not be on the winning side. This is an argument that appeals to many. So someone seeking to refute ISIS should not be strengthening their chief propaganda tool. But this cleric or any other cannot help but strengthen ISIS. All clerics believe in the same core theology as do the terrorists. These predictions come from Ahadith (purported sayings of the prophet, pl. of Hadith) and ulema (scholars) from all school of thought consider them akin to revelation. These end-time prophesies can only by questioned fruitfully by questioning the credibility of narrations that were collected up to 300 years after the demise of the Prophet and attributed to him, not by calling them akin to revelation.

Some of these prophesies also come from speculative readings of two allegorical verses in the Quran 4:159; 43:61. Muslims have been asked not to speculate about their meaning and leave them alone. But, of course, Muslims do, and the result is prophesied scenarios of apocalyptic wars. Similarly, in its core theology even the 14,000-word fatwa issued recently (August 2015) by 120 scholars from around the world, agrees with the militant ideologies. Their "Open Letter to Al-Baghdadi" also calls Hadith akin to revelation, knowing full well that all justifications of killings of innocent civilians come from a hadith attributing to the Prophet permission for killing of innocents in an attack at Taif by the use of catapult (manjaniq): (Sahih Muslim 19: 4321 & Sahih Bukhari 4: 52:256). This hadith is also used by al-Qaeda to justify use of weapons of mass destruction.

In point 16. Hudud (Punishment), the moderate fatwa establishes a general rule: "Hudud punishments (death for apostasy, etc.) are fixed in the Qur'an and Hadith and are unquestionably obligatory in Islamic Law." Having accepted the basic premise of the Baghdadi tribe it goes on to criticise its implementation in the so-called Islamic State. But once moderate ulema have accepted the basic premise of Hudud (Punishments) based on some verses of Quran and seventh century Bedouin tribal Arab mores being "unquestionably obligatory in Islamic Law," what difference does actually remain between moderation and extremism?

In point 20 of the fatwa, the moderate ulema seem to be justifying the destruction of idols and Sufi shrines, by talking of the supposed Islamic obligation to destroy and remove all manifestations of shirk (idolatry), only opposing the destruction of graves of the prophets and their companion.

In point 22 of the Open Letter, titled, The Caliphate, the moderate ulema again concur with the basic proposition of the Baghdadi clique: "There is agreement (ittifaq) among scholars that a caliphate is an obligation upon the Ummah. The Ummah has lacked a caliphate since 1924 CE."

This moderate fatwa even expresses belief in the theory of abrogation, whereby terror ideologues debunk peaceful Meccan verses that came at the beginning of Islam. Thus, like Sheikh Yaqoobi's "Refuting ISIS" this fatwa too strengthens the terrorist ideology, while criticising its practice.

This is not surprising. The commonly accepted theology of most Muslims agrees with the following features of the jihadist theology:

- It regards God as an implacable, anthropomorphic figure permanently at war with those who do not believe in His uniqueness, as against the Sufi or Vedantic concept of God as universal consciousness or universal intelligence radiating His grace from every atom in the universe.
- Quran as an uncreated aspect of God, a copy of the eternal Book lying in the Heavenly vault. Hence all its verses, in their literal meaning, have to be treated as an eternal guidance to Muslims without any reference to context.
- Ahadith or so-called sayings of Prophet Mohammad (pbuh) as akin to revelation, even though they were collected two to three hundred years after the demise of the Prophet. This is what allows ISIS to justify civilian killings and sex with female war prisoners. It also helps ISIS draw an apocalyptic, end-time war scenario and attract Muslim youth to participate in what they are told is a final war to make Islam victorious in the world;
- Sharia laws as divine, even though they were first codified 120 years after God announced the completion of the religion in one of the last verses in Quran.
- Jihad in the sense of Qital (warfare) as the sixth pillar of Islam.
- Some early verses of Quran have been abrogated and replaced by better and more appropriate later verses. This consensual doctrine of abrogation is used by radical ideologues to claim all 124 foundational, Meccan verses of peace, pluralism, co-existence with other religious communities, compassion, kindness to neighbours, etc., have been abrogated and replaced by later Medinan verses of war, xenophobia and intolerance.
- Hijra (migration to Darul Islam—abode of Islam—from Darul

Harb (Land of disbelief and conflict) as a religious duty and an act of devotion.

- A caliphate is an obligation upon the Ummah (global Muslim community).

Twentieth century scholars like Syed Qutb (1906–1966) of Egypt's Muslim Brotherhood and Abul A'la Maududi (1903–1979), of India and later Pakistan, who founded Jamaat-e-Islami, are considered the two fathers of modern Islamist terrorism or jihadism. More contemporary ideologues who have contributed enormously to the jihadist discourse are Abdullah Yusuf Azzam (1941-89) and Abu Muhammad al Maqdisi (Born: 1959), etc. Many Muslim scholars would distance themselves from these militant scholars today. But the reason jihadism is so influential and attractive to so many is that the jihadist theology is based on the popular theology propounded by major classical Arab theologians like Ibn-e-Taimiya (1263-1328), and Mohammad Ibn-e Abdul Wahhab (1703-1792) or for that matter major Indian theologians like Mujaddid Alf-e-Saani Shaykh Ahmad Sirhindī (1564-1624) and Shah Waliullah Dehlavi (1703-1762).

For hundreds of years now, major Muslim theologians have been engaged in creating a coherent and comprehensive theology of supremacism, intolerance and violence in order to expand the Islamic reach. They have conclusively made the lower form of jihad, i.e., warfare, compulsory for Muslims in place of the highest form of jihad which calls for struggle against one's own lower self. Luminaries of Islam have established a theology which basically declares that Islam must conquer the world and it is the religious duty of all Muslims to strive towards that goal and contribute to it in whatever way they can. All these theologians present in essence a supremacist, exclusivist, xenophobic and intolerant view of Islam and wield enormous influence on our clergy today.

It is not possible to accept classical theologians and reject their modern militant offshoots just as it is not possible to reject Abu Bakr al-Baghdadi and accept Zakir Naik simply because the latter is not actually having sex with sex slaves as Baghdadi is. Our radicalised youngsters can very well see the hypocrisy of those who on the one hand revere Taimiya, Wahhab, Sirhindi and Waliullah and on the other hand claim to oppose Qutb, Maududi, Azzam and Maqdisi and their followers like Osama bin Laden and Abu-Bakr al-Baghdadi. No surprise that some of our educated, 21st century, internet generation youth choose to rather be honest terrorists than dishonest hypocrites like their parents, community leaders, politicians, madrasa teachers, mosque imams, intellectuals, etc. who keep saying Islam is a religion of peace while also professing belief in the core theology of jihadism, equating it with Islam.

One of the key instructions of God was moderation in matters of religion (Quran: 4:171 and 5:80). This was repeated often by the Prophet: "Beware of extremism in religion, for it destroyed those before you." [Sahih al-Jami' (nos. 1851 & 3248), M.N. al-Albani, no. 2680, and & al-Sahihah of M.N. al-Albani, no. 1283.] But extremism has been endemic in Islam, present almost from the beginning of Islamic history. Muslims fought among themselves and quite vehemently, even before the collection of Hadith which they now consider divine, and codification of Sharia which they consider their religious duty to impose on the world. Muslims have still not found an antidote to militant verses in the Quran. Considering all verses of Quran as providing eternal guidance undermines the universality of essential, foundational, constitutive, verses that were revealed largely in the initial years of Islam in Mecca. We received very good advice from Pope Francis recently (September 2015) which is consistent with several verses in the Quran. Describing the holy Quran as a "prophetic book of peace," Pope Francis asked Muslims to seek "an adequate interpretation." The Quran also asks Muslims repeatedly to reflect upon the verses and find their best meaning, as in Chapter 39: verse 55; 39: 18; 39: 55; 38: 29; 2: 121; 47: 24, etc.

Calling Hadith and Sharia divinely inspired and fundamental elements of Islamic faith is irrational. Saying that it is a Muslim's primary religious duty to help establish God's sovereignty on earth and impose "divine" Sharia laws on the globe is only a way to intensify extremism which goes against the basic tenets of Islam. The idea of jihad against kuffar and hijrat (emigration) to the so-called Islamic State as a religious duty is preposterous at a time when millions of Arab Muslims are marching almost barefoot to Europe, the so-called Darul Harb, seeking refuge, a refuge that is denied to them by the so-called Darul Islam in the Arab world.

Muslims will just have to abandon the generally accepted current theology that leads to violence and supremacism. We will need to revisit all our literature, even popular fiction and romance, and explain to our youth that we are now living in a multicultural, multi-religious world where a binary thinking of Muslim/kafir as opposites and permanent war with them or self-segregation is just not viable. Even Saudi Arabia, which teaches in its schools the worst forms of intolerance, xenophobia, supremacism and exclusivism, has to deal with all religious communities.

ISIS may be militarily defeated tomorrow and even go out of existence. But this will not solve the problem of Muslim radicalisation. If our madrasas and educational institutions continue to prepare the ground for self-segregation and militancy, expounding the current theology, mixed with narratives of victimhood and marginalisation, Islam will continue to be hobbled, Muslims will continue to struggle to fit in the way of life in contemporary world. Moderate, progressive Muslims must urgently evolve and propagate an alternative theology of peace and pluralism, human rights and gender justice, consistent in all respects with the teachings of Islam, and suitable for contemporary and future societies, while refuting the current theology of violence and supremacism.

Unfortunately, as we have seen above, the task is not so easy. Radicalisation has not just happened overnight. Jihadi theology has evolved over hundreds of years. Major theologians who have studied Islam independently have brought to us a political version of Islam, stripping the religion of all its spirituality.

While it is primarily the duty of Muslims to fight this ideological war within Islam, this is no longer just a Muslim concern. The world too must confront Muslim scholars with the supremacism and extremism present in their theology and ask them to rethink. Progressive Muslims should join the rest of the world to defeat extremism in current, generally accepted Islamic theology. Islam has all the required resources to evolve a theology of peace and pluralism suited for the present age if only we read our scriptures differently and correctly, in accordance with repeated Quranic advice to find the best meaning of verses.

20

Regional and International Response to Global Terror

Lisa Curtis

The global terrorist threat has evolved and expanded since the death of Osama bin Laden nearly five years ago. In just the last three months, there have been major terrorist attacks throughout the world, most notably the November 13, 2015, attacks in Paris that killed 130. The so-called Islamic State (ISIS or ISIL) was responsible for the Paris attacks, as well as attacks in Istanbul, Jakarta, and Ouagadougou in early January. The December 2, 2015, shootings in San Bernardino, California, while probably not directed by ISIS (or al-Qaeda), were almost certainly inspired by the ideology of one or both of these groups.

Al-Qaeda—the rival, parent organisation of ISIS—is adapting its tactics and strategy to try to recover from an intensive U.S. drone campaign in Pakistan's tribal border areas that eliminated numerous al-Qaeda leaders, particularly from 2010-2012. Al-Qaeda has delegated command and control to affiliate organisations throughout the broader Middle East, and there are far more al-Qaeda affiliates operating throughout the world today than ever before. Some analysts have called this diffusion of the threat the beginning of a "global Islamist insurgency." Instead of being a centralised cadre of terrorists with tight command and control, al-Qaeda is now a loose network of groups operating across the globe.

Both al-Qaeda and ISIS constitute major threats to global security, but at present ISIS poses the most significant and immediate threat to international stability. Since June 2014 when it took control of Iraq's second largest city of Mosul and declared the establishment of a caliphate in areas under its control, ISIS has spread its tentacles throughout the Middle East, South and Southeast Asia, and Africa. Whether capturing swathes of territory (as in Iraq, Syria, and Libya); commanding allegiance from local militant groups (as in Afghanistan, Bangladesh, and Egypt); or recruiting foreign fighters to its cause from places like Saudi Arabia, Turkey, and Tunisia, ISIS has demonstrated its global reach and influence.

ISIS has also taken the terrorism phenomenon to new levels of depravity and violence. It has codified sexual slavery of women and girls mostly from the Yazidi minority community. The group's strategy also includes the dissemination of videos of gruesome murders of journalists, aid workers, and even rival militant factions, to both create fear in the populations under its control and to recruit more ruthless individuals to its cause.

ISIS Foreign Fighter Phenomenon

ISIS has been able to attract more than 25,000 foreign fighters—including over 4,500 from western nations—to join its ranks in Iraq and Syria. Through a sophisticated Internet and social media campaign, ISIS leaders have convinced an unprecedented number of individuals to leave their home countries to fight for the caliphate. Individual motivations for joining ISIS vary widely among individuals and in different regions of the world. The civil war in Syria was initially the main catalyst for young people to travel to the Middle East to fight the regime of Syrian dictator Bashar al-Assad. Failure of Western nations to respond to incidents like Assad's 2013 chemical attack on civilians facilitated ISIS recruiting.

While some individuals are motivated primarily by religion, others are seeking a source of identity and desire to commit to a cause larger than themselves. Some ISIS recruits are simply psychopathic, seeking adventure and the opportunity to commit violence. In Western Europe, ISIS often connects through social media with

Muslim immigrants who may feel marginalised from society. ISIS recruiters work to further isolate these individuals and then brainwash them into believing it is their religious duty to join and fight for the caliphate in Syria and Iraq.

The complexity of the recruitment process and varying motivations for joining ISIS help explain why it has been so difficult for countries throughout the world to stem the rising tide of radicalisation.

Threats to U.S.

ISIS has already inspired several attacks in the U.S. The most notable was last December's shootings in San Bernardino, California, carried out by Syed Rizwan Farook and Tashfeen Malik that killed 14. The investigations into the attacks so far show that Farook and Malik had been radicalised for some time and were likely inspired by both al-Qaeda and ISIS ideology. Malik had sent private messages on social media to Pakistani friends as early as 2012 declaring her support for jihad. Farooq was an American of Pakistani origin, whose parents had recently divorced.

In addition to the San Bernardino attacks, there have been several other terrorist incidents inspired by ISIS's ideology and message, such as Zale Thompson's hatchet attack on New York City police officers in October 2014. On May 3, 2015, there was a foiled attack by two Islamist extremists who were fatally shot by police before they could commit mass murder at a contest to draw the Prophet Muhammad in Garland, Texas.

FBI Director James Comey reported last year that tracking Americans who have returned from Syria is one of the FBI's top counterterrorism priorities, and that the FBI is currently investigating suspected ISIS supporters in all 50 states. In 2015 alone, the FBI foiled at least 11 Islamist terrorist plots against the U.S. homeland, more than in any other year since 9/11.

Countering Extremist Ideology and the Homegrown Threat

While denying terrorists the ability to control territory and enjoy safe haven is critical, it is equally important to actively counter the Islamist ideology that motivates the violence. The Obama administration has been reluctant to talk about the ideological underpinnings of terrorism and the relationship between Islamism (political Islam) and terrorism. Counterterrorism policies must take into account the direct connection between Islamist ideology and the terrorist attacks that are born of it. It would be impossible to uproot support for Islamist extremist ideology unless there is willingness among political leaders to discuss it candidly.

The democratic uprisings throughout the Arab world over the last five years have brought Islamist political parties to the fore, most notably in Egypt, where the Islamist Muslim Brotherhood held power from 2012-2013. While Islamist parties fill a political need and thus have a role to play in the democratic evolution of their respective countries, the anti-West ideologies and anti-democratic practices of the hardline elements among them pose serious risks to U.S. foreign policy objectives.

Islamists often pursue policies that undermine individual freedoms and lead to discrimination, repression, and violence against religious minority groups and women. Moreover, their lenient policies toward terrorist groups undercut U.S. counterterrorism measures and encourage a permissive environment for extremists to plot, plan, and train for international terrorist attacks. For instance, former Egyptian President and Muslim Brotherhood leader Muhammad Morsi, during his brief stint in power, released scores of terrorists from jail and called on the U.S. to release Sheikh Omar Abdel Rahman, who orchestrated the 1993 attack on the World Trade Centre. When Islamist party Ennahda held power in Tunisia from 2011 to 2014, thousands of Islamist extremists were released from jail, including Abu Iyad, who fought with al-Qaeda in Afghanistan. Once released, Iyad formed Ansar al-Sharia Tunisia (AST), a Salafist organisation adhering to al-Qaeda's ideology. AST was banned in Tunisia in August 2013 after the organisation was directly linked to two high-profile political assassinations.

For its part, the U.S. is grappling with how best to counter Islamic radicalism and homegrown terrorism without trampling on Muslim civil liberties. A report published by the New York Police Department

(NYPD) in 2007, "Radicalisation in the West: The Homegrown Threat," produced a backlash from the Muslim community in New York, which viewed its conclusions as justifying racial profiling. The NYPD report proposed ways to counter domestic radicalisation and thwart homegrown terrorist plots by "lone wolves" (individuals who conceptualise and carry out attacks on their own but are inspired by al-Qaeda—and increasingly ISIS—ideology). The report makes a case for identifying the threat at the point radicalisation begins, rather than after planning for an attack is underway. The NYPD later distanced itself from the report's findings and agreed to remove the report from its web site as part of a settlement of a lawsuit that claimed Muslims were the target of baseless surveillance and investigations.

CNN National Security Analyst and Vice President of the New America Foundation Peter Bergen, in a recent article in the Wall Street Journal, discusses what he views as the differences between the counterterrorism strategy laid out in the 2007 NYPD report and the current FBI approach, which relies on behaviours of individuals—not the ideologies that may be driving them—to lead their investigations.

Still, RAND expert Cheryl Bernard, in her recent article in the National Interest, makes a strong case for paying attention to an individual's ideological orientation and the degree to which he/she is integrated into the local society. Bernard notes that Islamists who disavow violence still may contribute to the radicalisation process in that they believe Muslims living in the West should not integrate with Western values nor feel compelled to demonstrate loyalty to Western institutions. Bernard says, "They may be against violence, but they are also against integration." Given that ISIS preys on young Muslims in western countries who may feel disaffected or alienated within their societies, such Islamist policies would seem only to foster the radicalisation process.

Thwarting homegrown terrorist plots in the U.S. requires both an understanding of Islamist extremist ideology and how it drives terrorism and a recognition that the religion of Islam itself is not responsible for terrorism, but rather individual human beings who act in its name. Such distinctions are enormously important in upholding the U.S. commitment to religious freedom and in showing respect for the vast majority of peaceful American Muslims. It is essential that U.S. law enforcement officers reach out and work closely with American Muslim communities as they move forward with counter-radicalisation efforts. Fear-mongering about the religion of Islam—aside from being morally repugnant—undercuts counter-terrorism strategy by alienating Muslim communities, which can help identify threats before they materialise.

Pakistan and Terrorism

The global terrorist threat emanating from Pakistan remains a core U.S. national security concern as a multitude of different extremist groups with varying degrees of ties to al-Qaeda operate in and from Pakistan. Terrorist groups like the Lashkar-e-Taiba (LeT), which conducted the 2008 Mumbai attacks; Jaish-e-Mohammad (JeM), which carried out the January 2, 2016, attack on the Indian air base at Pathankot; and the Haqqani Network, which regularly conducts attacks in Afghanistan, all maintain links to the Pakistani security establishment and continue to operate relatively freely in the country.

Like the attempted bombing of Times Square in May 2010 by Faisal Shahzad, the San Bernardino attacks also have a link to Pakistan. Shahzad had received training at a terrorist camp in Pakistan's tribal border areas and was reportedly directed by the Tehrik-e-Taliban Pakistan (TTP or Pakistani Taliban) to carry out the attack. For her part, Tashfeen Malik attended a conservative women's school in the Punjab province and lived as a child in Saudi Arabia. There are some media reports indicating that Malik was linked to the famous Red Mosque in the heart of Islamabad. In 2007, the Pakistan military battled its own people at the Red Mosque to end a standoff with extremists. The showdown helped spawn the TTP, which has killed thousands of Pakistani civilians and security forces in terrorist attacks throughout the country.

Despite the Pakistani military campaign against TTP bases in North Waziristan that started over eighteen months ago, TTP retains the ability to strike Pakistani targets. On January 20th, militants stormed a university in the Pakistani city of Charsadda, killing 20 students and professors. TTP leader Umar Mansoor (mastermind of the 2014 attack on Peshawar Army Public School) claimed responsibility for the university attack on Facebook. Pakistani Director General of Inter-Services Public Relations Major General Asim Bajwa confirmed in a public statement that the attack was directed by Mansoor from a base in Afghanistan. Pakistan has arrested five suspects it says provided shelter, transport, and weapons to the four university attackers, who were killed on the scene.

The attack in Charsadda followed closely on the heels of the JeM attack on the Indian air base, which left seven Indian soldiers dead. Indian officials promptly provided their Pakistani counterparts information on the Pathankot attackers, making clear future Indo-Pakistani dialogue would hinge on whether Islamabad took decisive action on the leads.

The leader of JeM, Masood Azhar, spent time in an Indian jail but was released in 1999 to end a hijacking stand-off. He received a hero's welcome upon his return to Pakistan and then established the JeM, which was blamed for the December 2001 attack on the Indian parliament that led to a six-month military stand-off between India and Pakistan. Azhar lay low for several years after the 2003 Indo-Pakistani ceasefire took effect, but resurfaced in early 2014 to address a large public rally, where he called on suicide attackers to resume jihad against India.

There are questions about whether the Pakistan military may have had some hand in the Pathankot attack, given its past links to the JeM and its failure to restrict Masood Azhar's activities. This would seem counterproductive from the perspective that the Pakistan Army already has its hands full conducting counterinsurgency operations on its western flank along the border with Afghanistan. Still, the onus is on the Pakistan military and civilian leadership to track down the leads provided by New Delhi and to take action against the group and individuals involved in the attack.

Pakistan has reportedly arrested several JeM militants, including leader Masood Azhar, but there is skepticism about whether Azhar will remain in custody. He was taken into custody shortly after the attack on the Indian parliament in 2001, but alter released. Pakistan has a poor track record of prosecuting terrorists, even those involved in attacks that have killed U.S. citizens. In April 2015, Pakistan released on bail the LeT mastermind behind the Mumbai attacks, Zakiur Rehman Lakhvi. The day before Lakhvi's release, the U.S. had announced the approval of nearly $1 billion in U.S. military sales to Pakistan. There were 166 victims in the Mumbai attacks, including six U.S. citizens. Family members of four of the U.S. victims filed a wrongful death lawsuit in a New York City court in 2010, accusing Pakistani intelligence of complicity in the Mumbai attacks.

While Pakistan has assisted the U.S. in capturing numerous al-Qaeda leaders, its support to groups like the Afghan Taliban, Haqqani network, LeT, and JeM, has undermined U.S. national security interests in the region and provided a conducive ideological environment for international terrorism to thrive in the country. Pakistan will only be able to fully get a handle on the terrorism problem within its own borders when its leadership repudiates and uproots the Islamist extremist ideology that drives all of these groups.

Al-Qaeda-ISIS Competition in South Asia

ISIS is seeking to make inroads into South Asia and in January 2015 announced the formation of the Khorasan group. Khorasan is an Islamic historical term used to describe the area encompassed by Afghanistan, parts of Pakistan, and parts of other countries bordering Afghanistan. According to the Hadith (sayings attributed to the Prophet Muhammad), South-Central Asia maintains a key role in establishing a global caliphate. The Hadith contains references to the Ghazwa-e-Hind (Battle of India), where the final battle between Muslims and non-Muslims before the end times will supposedly take place. One Hadith further says that an army with black flags will emerge from Khorasan to help the "Mahdi" (the prophesied redeemer of Islam) establish his caliphate at Mecca.

ISIS-Khorasan (ISIS-K) has been able to seize pockets of territory from the Taliban in the eastern Afghan province of Nangarhar, where the Pentagon says it has a presence of between 1,000 and 3,000 fighters. ISIS-K also is broadcasting radio programs in local languages in the region to recruit young Afghans. The propaganda denigrates both the Afghan government by portraying it as a puppet of the U.S. and the Taliban by claiming it has been co-opted by Pakistan.

ISIS-K is taking advantage of splits within the Taliban leadership that followed news last summer that Taliban supreme leader Mullah Omar had died over two years ago. One breakaway faction accuses the newly appointed Taliban leader, Mullah Akhtar Mansour, of lying about the circumstances surrounding Omar's death and of being too close to Pakistani intelligence. The U.S. recently formally designated ISIS-K as a terrorist organisation and gave greater leeway to U.S. forces to attack ISIS-K positions in Afghanistan.

ISIS faces obstacles in building bases in Afghanistan or Pakistan, primarily because al-Qaeda has well-established roots in the region and commands loyalty from the various South Asian terrorist organisations. Al-Qaeda leader Ayman al-Zawahiri has carefully nurtured the group's relationship with the Afghan Taliban, and publicly pledged his allegiance to Mullah Omar's successor, Mullah Akhtar Mansour, last August.

Zawahiri has also sought to make inroads with Muslim populations in other parts of South Asia to help fend off ISIS encroachment. In September 2014, Zawahiri made a video announcement launching an al-Qaeda wing in the Indian Subcontinent (AQIS). In the video, Zawahiri assures Muslims in India, Bangladesh, and Burma that the organisation "did not forget you and that they are doing what they can to rescue you from injustice, oppression, persecution, and suffering."

Way Forward

The U.S. must lead a multi-pronged, multi-nation effort to defeat ISIS by denying them the ability hold territory, disrupting their recruitment efforts, and countering their destructive ideology. The U.S. and its international partners must demonstrate that ISIS is not invincible. Without territory, ISIS cannot claim to have a caliphate.

This will require a robust military campaign, with much more intensive air strikes, expanded deployments of special operations forces, and the deployment of U.S. advisers embedded with the Iraqi army, Kurdish militias, and Sunni Arab militias. NATO allies are already showing a willingness to increase their military efforts due to the November 2015 Paris terrorist attacks—but they are looking to the U.S. to lead the effort.

Blocking terrorist travel also is a priority, especially given concerns about radicalised foreign fighters returning to their home countries to conduct attacks. The House of Representatives Homeland Security Committee Task Force report on foreign fighters that was released last September laid out numerous recommendations for countering terrorist travel. The report suggests that the U.S. government do more to share information on terrorist travel with international partners; to bolster law enforcement in dealing with the growing threat; and to enhance community awareness about the problem of youth radicalisation.

Just as it must lead the global military effort, the U.S. must also spearhead a global approach to countering the ideology that drives people to join ISIS. To do this, the U.S. needs a strong counter narrative that acknowledges the dangers to democracy of the Islamist agenda, including its persecution of religious minorities, repression of women, and support for Sharia law. The Obama administration has failed to lead the way in developing an effective counter narrative and has instead placed political correctness over precisely naming the threat.

One important way of undermining ISIS credibility and ideology is to amplify the stories of ISIS defectors. Most of the defectors have complained about the brutality that ISIS waged against fellow Sunnis, or have expressed their disillusionment with the factional infighting among the different extremist groups. While those who fought for ISIS should face the legal consequences, they should also be encouraged to tell their stories of disappointment and disillusionment.

Also important to countering the ideology is to convince the Saudi religious establishment to stop promoting its Wahhabist doctrine that inculcates hatred of other religious groups, including Christians, Jews and non-Sunni Islamic sects. This intolerant Sunni chauvinism leaves young Saudis open to the hostile ideological propaganda disseminated by ISIS and al-Qaeda.

While individual countries will need to take responsibility for protecting their own homelands, there must be constant efforts among like-minded nations to share best practices and cutting-edge technologies that help thwart terrorist attacks. In the U.S., the FBI Joint Terrorism Task Force (JTTF), which is made up of local, state, and federal officials, has helped disrupt several attempted attacks. Better coordination among local and federal officials and among the various intelligence-gathering agencies has contributed to the U.S. ability to disrupt and prevent nearly 70 terrorist plots in the U.S. since the 9/11 attacks.

With regard to South Asia, the U.S. should foster continued support for NATO and U.S. counterinsurgency strategies in Afghanistan to prevent the Taliban from regaining influence in the region. The fall of the northern Afghan city of Kunduz to the Taliban in September 2015 demonstrated that the Afghan security forces continue to need U.S. and NATO support in the form of air strikes, intelligence, training, and battlefield advice. Afghan forces were able to regain control of Kunduz, but other key urban areas remain under threat from the Taliban.

Finally, and perhaps most importantly, the U.S. must continue to pressure the Pakistani government to shut down Pakistan-based terrorist groups such as the Haqqani Network, LeT, and JeM. These groups not only undermine stability and key U.S. national security interests in the region, they have been responsible for the deaths of several American civilian and military personnel.

Overcoming the terrorist threat emanating from within Pakistan will require Islamabad to rethink how it promotes its regional interests. Relying on terrorist proxies to undermine stability in neighboring states has backfired on Pakistan in the form of TTP attacks that have killed nearly 35,000 Pakistanis in the last decade. The Pakistani government's ambivalence toward the various Islamist terrorist groups has led to confusion in the minds of the Pakistani public, and made it difficult to rally public support behind military operations against groups like the TTP that attack the Pakistani state.

The Obama administration has wisely begun to condition aid to Pakistan on its cracking down on terrorist groups attacking U.S.

interests in Afghanistan. The administration last year withheld $300 million in Coalition Support Funds (CSF–reimbursement payments for Pakistani military deployments and operations along the border with Afghanistan) because of Pakistan's failure to meet legislative conditions on U.S. military aid, which include cracking down on Haqqani network bases within Pakistani territory.

For the U.S. to achieve its counterterrorism objectives in South Asia, it should continue to employ a mix of incentives and disincentives aimed at convincing Pakistan to widen its terrorist crackdown to all Islamist terrorist groups within its borders. Conditioning military aid to Pakistan may not constitute the silver bullet to gaining Islamabad's full counterterrorism cooperation, but at least it will ensure U.S. taxpayer money is not indirectly benefiting those terrorist groups seeking harm against the United States.

21

Global Terror and Impact on South Asia

Christian Wagner

The emergence of the Islamic State (IS)/Daesh and its rapid spread poses a serious challenge to the regional order in West Asia and beyond. Militant Islamic groups in different parts of the world, from Africa to Southeast Asia have pledged allegiance to the new caliphate. Terror attacks in Europe, Africa and different parts of Asia have underlined the danger that emanates from this new form of global terrorism.

The countries of South Asia have always struggled with different forms of global terrorism. The region is characterised by two paradoxes. The first is, that on the one hand, South Asia traditionally belongs to the most affected regions by terrorism in global comparison together with the Middle East and North Africa (MENA) and Sub-Sahara Africa. But, on the other hand, the security situation has improved for most countries in the region. Overall, there is a decrease in the number of fatalities by terrorism from over 29,000 in 2009 to 4,477 in 2015. In Pakistan, the number of terrorist incidents came down by 48 percent in 2015 compared to the previous year with a total number of 625 terrorist attacks. In India, the Home Ministry noted that the internal security situation showed a "significant improvement" in 2014-15. Afghanistan is the only South Asia country where the security situation has further deteriorated in recent years. Reports indicate that the Taliban got their widest reach since 2001. In 2015, half of the districts in the country had a "high" or "extreme" threat level. "27 of Afghanistan's 34 provinces had some districts where the threat level was rated high or extreme."

The second paradox is that regardless of the fact that South Asia is home of nearly half the Muslim population worldwide and militant organisations like Al-Qaeda and Islamic State have always targeted South Asian countries, the propaganda of the IS hardly resonates among South Asian Muslims. In contrast, the propaganda of the Islamic State falls on a much more fertile ground in Europe. Several thousand fighters from Europe have joined the Islamic State and many of them have already returned home, posing a new security challenges to European societies. Compared to these figures the number of arrested IS supporters in India is still below one hundred people although India has a Muslim population of more than 13 percent, i.e. more than 150 million people.

In order to analyse the impact of global terrorism on the region, the article will first look at the changing character of terrorism in South Asia. The second part will look at some of the strategies on how South Asian countries have tried to tackle terrorism and its root causes.

Changing Character of Global Terrorism: From Ethnic Separatism to Religious Fundamentalism

South Asia is plagued by different forms of militant groups which can be differentiated in three broad categories, i.e. left wing extremism (LWE), ethnic separatism, and religious fundamentalism. All groups have used terrorism as an instrument for their struggle. The various forms of militancy also had different international repercussions over time.

The militant communist groups had international support in the beginning. The communist rebellion in Telangana in the 1950s was supported by the Communist International, and the beginnings of the Maoist movement in the late 1960s was supported by China. In the 1990s and 2000s the Maoist movements in India and Nepal started to cooperate in order to establish a "red corridor". With the political integration of the Maoists in Nepal and the decline of the Maoist movement in India, the threat has decreased, but it remains virulent in some states and districts in India. Today, there is hardly any international support for this form of militancy.

Various ethnic separatist groups in South Asia have relied on regional and international support both by states and their diaspora networks. The Liberation Tigers of Tamil Eelam (LTTE) was regarded as one of the most successful militant organisations until its military defeat in May 2009. Initially, the LTTE enjoyed state support by the Indian government in Delhi as well as by different state governments in Tamil Nadu. After the failure of the Indian Peace Keeping Force (IPKF) between 1987 and 1991, the LTTE was able to continue its struggle by its global network among the Tamil diaspora that stretched from Southeast Asia, South Africa to Europe and North America. Following the terror attacks of 9/11, a variety of new international regulations have been passed in order to control its financial flows. This has also affected many separatist groups and their regional and international networks. But ethnic separatism among the Baluch, Sikhs, Nagas, Madeshis, and Tamils continues to remain a challenge for many South Asian countries.

The latest and most serious challenge stems from militant Islamic groups which have different forms of international networks and support structures. For India, the most important challenge comes from groups like Lashkar-e-Taiba (LeT) and Jaish-e-Mohammed (JeM) and their charity organisations which enjoy state support by Pakistan despite international sanctions. The support has widely been analysed by international and Pakistani scholars. Former President Musharraf openly admitted that the Inter-Services Intelligence (ISI) had trained LeT and JeM. It would nevertheless be misleading to include all forms of Islamic militancy under the same category. Musharraf had pointed out, that the use of militant groups had always been instrumental in order to force India into negotiations over Kashmir. It remains an open question in how far all the groups are still under the control of the ISI or in how far factions have become independent.

Pakistan has also supported the Taliban in Afghanistan in order to pursue its foreign policy goals especially vis-à-vis India. With the creation of the TTP it became obvious that this strategy had backfired on the Pakistani state and its society. The military operation in North Waziristan in summer 2014 and the attack on the Army Public school in Peshawar in December 2014 have changed the discourse on the "good" and "bad" Taliban. But Pakistan's policy change will only be credible if the security forces also takes on militant groups like LeT and JeM.

The threat that emanates from groups like Al-Qaeda and IS/ Daesh falls under a different category. Both groups are targeting the West and the United States as well as their allies, among which are also Muslim states like Pakistan. Their goals, like the creation of a global caliphate and Islamisation on the basis of their interpretation of Sharia are not negotiable. They receive support by groups from within the Gulf region and are also able to attract international fighters by their social media campaigns.

Al-Qaeda and IS/Daesh have also targeted countries like India. Osama Bin Laden already threatened India in 1999 and in 2009 a senior Al-Qaeda leader again promised more attacks on India. IS / Daesh has also unilaterally declared war on India and has targeted the country for a major attack. But the propaganda and recruitment of both militant organisations has only provoked limited resonance among the Indian Muslims. India security forces have arrested a number of suspects with connections to IS/Daesh, however, the number of Indians who are reportedly fighting for IS in West Asia is much lower than the number of foreign fighters from Europe. Following media reports, 15 Indians are said to be active members of the IS in Syria, and six others have been killed fighting for the group. Nearly 35 persons, suspected to be IS sympathisers, have been sent back to India by various countries in recent times.

The presence of IS/Daesh in Afghanistan and Pakistan seems to be higher although there are no clear figures. As a result of internal conflict, various Taliban commanders in both countries have pledged their allegiance to the new group. Moreover, pamphlets and graffiti of IS supporters have been distributed in various parts of Pakistan. The security forces have also revealed IS cells in cities like Karachi and Lahore and have identified members who travelled to the Middle East in order to join IS. In Bangladesh, the IS claimed responsibility for the killing of several foreigners in 2015 but the government has dismissed these claims.

In contrast to previous forms of global terrorism, IS/Daesh poses a serious threat and has a new quality. First, it has a much stronger transnational foundation and less support by specific states. Second, it is able to mobilize its followers on a global level by its social media activities. This poses new challenges for states to tackle the problem.

Tackling Global Terrorism in South Asia

National Level: Tackling the Root Causes of Terrorism

It is a well-known fact that the fight against terrorism can only be won by political solutions rather than by military operations. The different forms of militancy address different grievances. Communist groups have mostly focused on the socio-economic inequalities, ethnic groups have demanded new forms of self-determination, autonomy or independence, while religious extremist groups are fighting for different order based on the imposition of religious laws both on the national, the regional and even on the global level.

One common denominator between the various grievances seems to be the lack of justice. Militant groups like the Taliban, the LTTE, and the Naxalites were able to get some form of support by providing justice and setting up some form of governance in those areas under their control. The establishment of better forms of governance and rule of law are therefore among the most important tasks in order to tackle militancy. South Asian governments have initiated a variety of programs and political reforms to address the root causes of militancy and terrorism in recent years. The Indian government has initiated various social schemes under the heading of "inclusive growth". The aim was to achieve a better distribution of economic growth but also to create new job opportunities, especially in remote rural districts which were affected by the Naxalites. The Mahatma Gandhi National Rural Employment Guarantee Act (MGNREGA), the Food Security Bill and the Right to Education Act were among the most prominent government schemes in recent years.

The demands of ethnic groups could be met with different forms of autonomy and federalism. The Indian government has used the instrument of state reorganisation to address the grievances of those groups especially in the Northeast. In Pakistan, the 18th amendment of 2010 will give the provinces more political responsibilities and financial opportunities once it is implemented. In Nepal, the question of ethnic or territorial federalism was the decisive factor in the process of constitution making after the end of the civil war. The Sri Lankan government missed the opportunity for a political solution after the end of the civil war in 2009. The new government of President Sirisena has decided to write a new constitution that will hopefully offer durable solutions for the question of autonomy and representation of the minorities.

The most difficult task is to find political solutions for religious extremism. The challenges are enormous not only for the Muslim countries in the region like Afghanistan, Pakistan, Bangladesh and the Maldives but also for secular countries like India. The role of religion in state and society is an ongoing controversial topic in most Muslim societies. The main challenge is that the demands for a more orthodox interpretation of religion by extremist groups are in contrast with the majority view. The great majority of Muslims in South Asia reject fundamentalist and extremist interpretations and instead prefer a more moderate role of religion. This is also underlined by the fact that Islamist parties in Pakistan and Bangladesh have never been able to attract a sizeable number of the electorate.

Secular societies like India face different challenges. The demands of Islamic extremist may provoke a counter reaction by Hindu extremist groups also against moderate members of the Muslim community. This may trigger a spiral of violence that will only help extremist forces on both sides but does not offer a political solution.

On the legal and law enforcement side the picture is mixed. Most South Asian governments have passed new security laws in order to handle terrorism. India has a variety of laws, for instance the Prevention of Terrorist Activities Act or the Unlawful Activities Prevention Act. Pakistan has enacted new legislation with the 21st amendment in January 2015 that was a reaction to the attack on the army public school in Peshawar in December 2014. Part of the new legislation was the setting up of military courts in order to deal with terrorist cases.

A much bigger challenge is the enforcement of these laws both by the judicial systems and by the police. Various studies and indicators show that South Asia is grossly under-policed in international comparison. In India the police/population ratio (per 100.000) is only 138 police men. This is far below the recommendations by the United Nations (UN) which are 220 men. Moreover, India's security establishment is still facing serious constraints on different levels with regard to equipment and training.

Comparisons among South Asian countries show a similar picture. There is only one police man for 304 persons in Pakistan, one for 568 persons in India, and one for 1,073 persons in Bangladesh. Moreover, most police forces in South Asia do not enjoy a very positive image among the population. Strengthening the police forces remains a paramount task, since they rather than the intelligence organisations are the first at the defence line in the fight against militancy.

Regional Security Cooperation in South Asia

An interesting side effect of the fight against (global) terrorism is the growing security cooperation in South Asia. This form of cooperation runs counter to the well-known argument, that South Asia is a region of "chronic instability" because of the various bilateral conflicts between India and her neighbours. India has initiated different instruments for security cooperation ranging from military and police training, joint operations, to intelligence sharing. A common feature of the different types of cooperation is that they are targeted against different militant groups no matter whether they have a regional or a global outreach.

Moreover, India and the neighbours have expanded their legal collaboration both on the bilateral and the multilateral level. India has signed Mutual Legal Assistance Treaties with Bangladesh, Sri Lanka, and Afghanistan. The Home Ministers have started common meetings on the SAARC level in 2005. In 2008, SAARC agreed on

Mutual Assistance in Criminal Matters. But this will come into force only after ratification by all members.

Global Efforts

The aftermath of the attacks of 9/11 brought a variety of new international efforts to fight terrorism and its support structures. Militant organisations have been banned, new international regulations have been passed to curb the financing of terrorist groups. One important institutions to coordinate the various efforts of the international community is the Counter-Terrorism Committee (CTC) of the Security Council. New challenges like IS have also led to new measures. In December 2015, the first meeting of the finance ministers took place on the level of the Security Council in order "to cut off all sources of funding for the Islamic State in Syria and Iraq (ISIL) and other terrorist groups...". India and Pakistan have also intensified their bilateral security cooperation with the United States, and European countries like the United Kingdom, France and Germany.

Prospects

Global Islamic terrorism in the form of IS/Daesh poses a new security threat for many countries. But, the relative low figures of followers and the small numbers of fighters from the region that have joined IS indicate that South Asia seems to be better prepared to cope with the challenge compared to other regions. First, most countries in the region seem to have developed a culture of moderation and tolerance between the religious communities, even if hardliners from different extremist are challenging this status quo. Second, regional security cooperation has increased so that there is a greater awareness of the potential threats. This does not imply to underestimate the challenge that emanates from IS/Daesh. But the more immediate security threats in the region do not come from global terrorism but rather from different regional militant groups and their state supporters.

22

Lessons Learnt from the Sri Lankan Experience of Countering Terrorism: A South Asian Perspective

Admiral (Dr.) Jayanath Colombage

In this article, I focus my attention only on the Sri Lanka experience against the Liberation Tigers of Tamil Eelam (LTTE). There is no doubt that terrorism has evolved into a worldwide phenomenon and it is here to stay. Terrorism has become the most dominant threat to world peace in this 21st century. No country in the world can be immune to the scourge of terrorism. The advanced, developed countries or pioneers of democracy are no longer safe from acts of terrorism. Despite the great efforts of law enforcement authorities, armed forces, enhanced surveillance, profiling, monitoring, the terrorist always finds ways and means of exploiting the systems and carrying out their dastardly acts. Presently the European Union and Middle East have become a playground for terrorists and soon it could move on to South and South East Asia.

Terrorists are now getting more and more brutal and they want more people killed and more people to see those being killed. They want maximum publicity to their brutal acts of terror. They not only kill innocent civilians by indiscriminate bombing but even by beheading, shooting at point blank range, burning alive, drowning in a cage; some of the methods which were used in medieval times. The terrorists do not spare anyone; even the small children who have not seen the world are targeted in order to convey their message. Kidnapping, hostage taking, raping, ethnic cleansing, religious based persecution are all part of the game for modern day terrorists. These terrorist acts result in the large scale migration of people to different parts of the world and this is a major concern for global security. The terrorists are willing to violate human rights without any consideration. The social media is being heavily exploited by terrorist groups, mainly for propaganda, recruitment and funding purposes. As the technological advances in the world have made it possible for people to be connected without any cost, in real time, terrorist groups use the same means to get connected to their target groups. The perception that democracies, good governance and prosperity do not breed terrorism is increasingly being challenged and we now see many affluent young men and women, even children from advanced and developed countries joining these terrorist groups.

The Case of Sri Lanka

Sri Lanka experienced a bitter, protracted and violent insurgency conflict for nearly three decades. It shattered the nation and tore apart the social fabric. Disharmony and suspicion among various ethnic communities grew to an unprecedented level. This conflict slowed down the economic progress of the country and affected its development badly. It destroyed property and many lives were lost too. It is estimated that during this conflict, an average of 350 lives were lost on a monthly basis. It also created a large scale refugee problem towards India and towards developed countries. It also resulted in regional and international mediation and intervention.

The economic loss due to the insurgency was huge. Defence expenditure was increased from 1.6 per cent GDP in 1983 to 5.9 per cent GDP in 2009. The cost incurred in the final stages of the war between 2005 and 2009 is estimated to be around 5.5 billion USD. This was a huge price for a developing country. This money could have been used for development and for the betterment of the population. The conflict slowed down the investment flow as new investors were not willing to come forward without peace and stability in the country.

This conflict resulted in a large number of casualties. The casualty figure for armed forces was 23327 killed and 60000 wounded in action whilst the estimate for LTTE stands at 27000 killed. There are conflicting figures given for civilian casualties. However, it could be as high a figure as 100000.

The LTTE

The LTTE was considered as the most ruthless terrorist organisation in the world until 2009 and now this title is taken over by the ISIS or Daesh. Suicide terrorism was considered as the trade mark of the LTTE. During the entire period of war the LTTE had carried out 378 suicide attacks; 274 by male cadres and 104 by female cadres. The LTTE invented and pioneered the suicide jacket and belt, suicide vehicle bombs, suicide boats, and a host of underwater improvised explosive devices. The female suicide bomber who killed a former Prime Minister of India, Sri Rajeev Gandhi wore a suicide jacket designed and perfected by the LTTE. The LTTE is the only terrorist organisation in the world which compelled all its members to wear a cyanide capsule around their neck to commit suicide if they ran the risk of getting arrested by the armed forces. This included about 6000 child combatants.

The LTTE killed a large number of politicians of all ethnic communities, the largest being from their own Tamil community. They also killed Tamil moderates, intellectuals, basically anyone who did not side with them. They are the only terrorist organisation in the world which has assassinated two international leaders, a President of Sri Lanka and a former Prime Minister of India. They attacked the international airport, Central Bank, many other economic and public targets and a large number of religious sites, sea ports and even places of worship in Sri Lanka. Sea ports were a high priority target and they launched attacks on all major ports including the port of Colombo, albeit with limited success. At times, ports were secured by having personnel manning coastal areas for about 30 kilometres either side in order to prevent any attacks being launched.

The LTTE also carried out ethnic cleansing by forcing the Sinhalese and Muslim population out of their intended separate state, Eelam.

Maritime Capability of the LTTE Sea Tigers

The LTTE is the only terrorist organisation to incorporate the maritime domain into their grand strategy. Normally terrorist organisations do not venture into the ocean or stay there for too long as it would give away the surprise element, which is essential to the success of their attacks. However, the LTTE developed their maritime wing called the Sea Tigers, similar to that of a navy. The Sea Tigers became a force to reckon with at sea, which is rare by any standards. They used the tactic of swarming naval targets with suicide boats to drive a point home that their cadres were fearless. They used the gains by the Sea Tigers as propaganda tools for recruitment and to raise funds especially from Tamil diaspora communities, by motivating them and further reinforcing the cause.

The Sea Tigers were also able to carry out maritime operations in the full domain of the maritime environment. They were engaged in large scale maritime crime activities such as piracy, hostage taking, surface and sub-surface attacks against naval and merchant vessels, mining the ocean routes, human smuggling, narcotic smuggling and large scale gun running. They operated 12-15 merchant vessels plying international shipping routes and docking in international sea ports by using the international maritime logistic system. They functioned like any other international shipping company by having front offices in many capitals of the world.

Further, the LTTE masterminded terrorist financing by exploiting the liberty given by the host countries and the money thus raised was used to purchase large quantities of military hardware from different parts of the world. Despite the common belief that terrorists acquire weapons from the black market, the LTTE bought weapons from the original manufacturers, through third party involvement by abusing the end user certificate. They were able to stockpile large quantities of war-fighting equipment and materials on board their fleet of merchant vessels and transport them to the Sri Lankan coastal areas under their control, from time to time. Two question begging answers in this regard are: How was it possible for the LTTE to buy large quantities of war fighting items and use international ports and shipping lanes to transport them despite various international control regimes and protocols? If a relatively small organisation like LTTE can do this, what about a much larger, trans-national terrorist organisation doing the same or even bigger scale gun running? It is worth mentioning that the LTTE was not only acquiring small arms and ammunition to wage a guerrilla war but conventional military equipment like long range artillery guns, mortars and ammunition for the same. This was for conventional war-fighting, in order to take over the country. They had a very clear grand strategy and they had almost achieved their objectives. There were border villages and forward defensive lines in Sri Lanka as we can see between two countries. The LTTE not only developed an effective de-facto navy but a mini air force too. These light aircraft were used to bomb a number of targets in the capital city Colombo and to return back to areas under their control safely.

The LTTE was capable of organising a sophisticated, well connected international network by exploiting the Tamil diaspora, which was used for fund raising and acquiring of war fighting materials. They raised funds through credit card fraud, passport forgery, drug trafficking, extortion and coercion. There were some legal businesses belonging to the group too. These were operating petrol/gas stations, schools, mass media institutes, grocery shops, gold shops and even charitable organisations. The Tamil diaspora could be divided into front and cover organisations of the LTTE and its sympathisers. Although the LTTE was defeated on the soil of Sri Lanka, these diaspora organisations still hope to achieve a separate state, Eelam, by political means.

Cease Fire Agreements and Negotiations

There were a number of attempts at negotiations, mediations and Cease Fire Agreements (CFA) during this conflict. The final CFA was from 2002 to 2005 with international monitoring carried out by Scandinavian monitors. There were large scale violations of this CFA by the LTTE. There were 3830 such violations by the LTTE in comparison with about 351 by armed forces. During these CFAs, the LTTE would systematically settle families of their intelligence cadres around military installations and other vital targets in order to gather necessary information. The LTTE leader threatened that if the government went into an offensive he would ensure a blood bath in the rest of the country. The LTTE was ready; they had positioned their cadres in strategic locations and placed weapons, ammunitions and explosives in vantage locations. However, this CFA broke the LTTE organisation into two as well. The eastern fighters separated from the LTTE and tried to form a separate entity and that helped the armed forces to exploit the situation to their advantage.

In concluding, it can be said that the LTTE was indeed greatly daring and ruthless, innovative and adoptive, skilful in the use of environment, exercised tactical proficiency and strategic mastery, were dedicated and committed to their cause and perfected the use of duel use technology in their battle plans.

Just War and Give War a Chance – Final War after 2005

In 2005, President Rajapaksa came to power with a mandate to eradicate terrorism in the country. Like on previous occasions, negotiations with the LTTE commenced. However, the LTTE was buoyant with their military gains and had an ability to attack any target at their will. Hence, the negotiations broke down and the CFA was hanging in the balance. Certain actions taken by the LTTE, compelled the government to engage in limited offensive operations. When the LTTE closed a sluice gate which was providing water to a large number of people in the eastern province, the government decided to go on the full offensive. When the latter forces started clearing the eastern province, the LTTE was not able to defend large stretches of land they were occupying. Soon, the East was liberated and there were simultaneous attacks launched by the Army in the Northern province too. The coordinated and simultaneous military offensive was too much for the LTTE to bear. They were losing ground which was once under their total control.

Meanwhile, the Sri Lanka Navy decided to go after the Sea Tigers and to attack the centre of gravity of the LTTE; their logistic network.

The navy, which did not have any blue water capability, ventured few thousand nautical miles from Sri Lanka and attacked the LTTE floating warehouses, which were used to stockpile the war-fighting materials in international shipping lanes far away from Sri Lanka. The navy regained the initiative at sea from the Sea Tigers. In addition, the air force was carrying out precision bombing at LTTE targets based on solid information. The once mighty LTTE was crumbling. They were losing the ability to sustain the battle. They were also not receiving the much needed logistics and were losing ground rapidly. They could not use heavy artillery or mortars and hence casualties to armed forces became less.

Likewise, the LTTE gradually became a spent force. The LTTE leadership was however not ready to commit suicide by swallowing cyanide capsules that they were wearing around their necks. They made a number of attempts to escape across land as well as sea. They had a grand plan to escape by sea. The LTTE international logistic mastermind, KP was ready with a merchant ship and a helicopter to evacuate the LTTE leadership. However, the navy had four layered barrier defence at sea. The LTTE sent a number of decoys but were captured by the navy. One boat carried the wife and family of Sea Tiger leader, who were later arrested and released.

Grand Victory and Eliminating Terrorism from Sri Lanka

For the government of Sri Lanka, this was a 'Just War'. It had to be fought. The LTTE had to be defeated. The war should be allowed to come to a logical conclusion so as to ensure lasting peace. Hence the government offensive continued despite some international pressure to stop it. On 19th May 2019, the grand victory was achieved and the LTTE leadership was killed in battle. The LTTE's ability to wage war in Sri Lanka was comprehensively defeated. Large stocks of war-fighting materials were later recovered buried underground. The armed forces quickly took control of the areas. Nearly 300,000 Tamil civilians who were used as a human shield by the LTTE were rescued and sent to IDP centres. These civilians have now been resettled, mostly in their original habitats. 12000 LTTE combatants were sent through a rehabilitation program and were reintegrated into society.

Development of the war torn areas commenced and the livelihoods of people were restored. The root-causes of the problem are being addressed through constitutional reforms and means. Sri Lanka was not caught in the 'conflict trap'. The theory of 'conflict trap' would argue that nearly after five years from a violent protracted conflict, violence is likely to return. But this did not happen in Sri Lanka. Now there is no terrorism in the country. No one is getting killed due to terrorism.

Conventional wisdom would argue that militaries should create conditions conducive for the application of a political solution so as to resolve an insurgency conflict. That is true and there is no doubt about this contention. However, the Sri Lankan case proved that given the right conditions, a decisive battle field victory is desirable and possible against an insurgency. Thence, Sri Lanka became the only country in this century, so far, to have successfully defeated terrorism by military means. Now Sri Lanka needs to win peace. This is also a very difficult processes the conflict had shattered the confidence between communities for a long period.

Determinants of Success: Lessons Learnt

There is no 'one size fits all' lessons from the Sri Lankan conflict. However, there can be many parallels which can be seen. From the defeat of terrorism in Sri Lanka, by countries suffering from the menace of terrorism. It is pertinent to identify the determinants of success in the Sri Lankan case. The most important determinant can be described as the Political leadership and resolve to end the war. Many political leaders from time to time attempted to find a solution to this conflict. Some preferred the political option whilst some preferred the military option and on most occasions it wavered between the two. But after 2005, there was a very clear political resolve and the political and military wills were synergised to the best possible level. Though there was a strong political leadership, it did not interfere with the tactics of the military. The political leadership spelled out the strategy and provided necessary inputs to the military, who could conduct the war against terror on its own.

Also another noteworthy contribution came from the invigorating military leadership. Then there was large scale increase of the armed forces personnel. The army was increased from about 100000 to 250000 whilst the navy was increased from 37000 to 56000. Similarly, the strength of the air force was increased up to about 37000. The quantum increase helped to dominate the newly liberated areas of the north and east by the army. The fighting columns of the army was then free to continue with the offensive operations without bothering about holding ground. That kept the LTTE on the continuous move and they were unable to settle down to a regular pattern. There was also an infusion of modern technology suited for this situation and required platforms and machinery were acquired for armed forces. There were many research and development projects undertaken by the armed forces with the help of professionals from universities, the private sector and that too contributed to the final outcome in a great manner.

The Sri Lankan armed forces have been trained and raised with a conventional mindset. The LTTE on the other hand were using asymmetric tactics with great success against the armed forces. There was a realisation that unless armed forces also engaged in asymmetric tactics, defeating the LTTE was difficult. Hence the armed forces also changed their training and tactics based on years of experience fighting with the LTTE. The results were immediate. It confused the LTTE and forced them to be on the defensive and their movements were restricted immensely.

Every military historian would emphasise the importance of strategy. For the first time in the conflict, there was a grand strategy rather than having piece-meal strategies. There was a clear end state; to defeat the LTTE militarily. Military plans were made accordingly and operations were conducted successively and simultaneously. The objectives were very clear and the military was confident that they had the full backing of the polity. Intelligence gathering, analysing and dissemination also played a key role in the outcome of the grand victory. All intelligence agencies were brought under a chief of national intelligence and they started sharing information, and soon a larger tactical picture developed for the conduct of operations by the military.

The navy developed a very successful intelligence network combining HUMINT and SIGINT effectively. There was assistance from friendly countries as well. Developing a complete tactical intelligence picture was now possible and the military was more confident of the information received as they became very reliable and accurate. Yet, victory was not achieved by the military alone. There was a need for a whole country, or a comprehensive approach to win the war. A national will needed to be developed and the support of all stake holders was necessary. This included the civil societies, the clergy, intellectuals, scientists, academics, and many other subject matter experts. This approach could be considered very important for democracies to fight the menace of terrorism. Strategic communication was effectively used to convey the right message to the masses and even to the international community and agencies. War reporting was carried out from the battle lines and it became credible and people started believing what the media was transmitting. The mass media campaign was able to unite the population to fight the war and to achieve victory. The armed forces personnel were highlighted as 'War Heroes'

Conclusions and Take Away Points for Tackling Global Terror

In conclusion, I intend to mention some take away points. The world need to be united in the battle against terrorism. Terrorism is global and hence it needs a global response. One needs to be prepared for war even when negotiating for peace. If the terrorist feels that you are weak or not ready, they will attack. The terrorist will always use the lull periods in battle such as CFAs to enhance their capabilities. The world needs to be sincere in its efforts in combatting terrorism. Double standards as we see in today's global context; that is fighting one group of terrorists on the one hand and supporting another group of terrorists on the other hand, is detrimental to the genuine battle against terror. There should be a genuine Global War against Terror.

There also needs to be a comprehensive approach to fight terrorism. The Military and law-enforcement authorities alone cannot fight this war successfully. All stake holders, including civil society groups, have a role to play. The faith leaders, parents, families, friends and peer groups, have a role to play in the counter radicalisation and de-radicalisation of the youth from being a prey for terrorist organisations. Legitimate grievances of people should be addressed. This must be matched with economic, educational and societal development. Quite often it can be observed that even after a violent protracted conflict has been ended, the grievances which started the conflict in the first place, have not been suitably addressed. People feel that as an injustice; corruption leaves them with no choice for improving the quality of their lives. People need to be given hope. Further, denying human rights only pays into the hands of terrorists. The final point is the need to share experiences, knowledge and best practices in countering terrorism by those who are targets or likely targets of terror. This will help countries to understand threats, possibilities and necessary counter measures to combat such situations effectively before conditions grow to a level which cannot be reversed.

List of Contributors

Shri Pranab Mukherjee assumed office as the 13th President of India on July 25, 2012, crowning a political career of over five decades of exemplary service to the nation in Government as well as Parliament. A man of humble origins, Shri Mukherjee was born in the small village of Mirati in Birbhum District of West Bengal as son of freedom fighters, Shri Kamada Kinkar Mukherjee and Rajlakshmi on December 11, 1935. Shri Mukherjee's father was a Congress leader who endured great hardship including being sent to jail several times for his role in India's struggle for independence. He acquired a Master's degree in History and Political Science as well as a degree in Law from the University of Kolkata. He then embarked on his professional life as a college teacher and journalist. Inspired by his father's contribution to the national movement, Shri Mukherjee, in 1969, plunged into full time public life following his election to the Upper House of the Parliament (Rajya Sabha).

A man of unparalleled experience in governance with the rare distinction of having served at different times as Foreign, Defence, Commerce and Finance Minister, he was elected to the Upper House of the Parliament (Rajya Sabha) five times from 1969 and twice to the Lower House of the Parliament (Lok Sabha) from 2004. A prolific reader, Shri Mukherjee has authored several books on the Indian economy and on nation building. The many awards and honours conferred on him include India's second highest civilian award, Padma Vibhushan in 2008, the Best Parliamentarian Award in 1997 and Best Administrator in India Award in 2011.

Dr. Abdullah Abdullah graduated from Naderia High School in 1976 and went on to study ophthalmology at Kabul's University Department of Medicine where he received an MBBS degree in 1983. During the Soviet invasion of Afghanistan and communist Democratic Republic of Afghanistan government from 1985 to 1986 he worked in the ophthalmology hospital for Afghan refugees in Peshawar. In September 1985, he became the head of the Health Department for the Panjshir Resistance Front, coordinating treatments and health care for the resistance fighters and the civilian population. He became a close associate and advisor to mujahideen commander Ahmad Shah Massoud in the Soviet–Afghan War. Following the capture of Kabul by the Taliban, the Northern Alliance was created under the leadership of Ahmad Shah Massoud and Dr. Abdullah became the United Front's Minister of Foreign Affairs. After the overthrow of the Taliban in 2001, and following the Afghan Presidential election, 2004, Abdullah was reappointed as Minister of Foreign Affairs for one year. After the Presidential election of 2014, Dr Abdullah Abdullah was appointed as the Chief Executive, Islamic Republic of Afghanistan.

Rajnath Singh, was born on 10 July 1951 in village Puttur in Uttar Pradesh. He secured a Masters degree in physics from Gorakhpur University and has been associated with the Rashtriya Swayamsevak Sangh (RSS) since 1964, when he was just 13 years old. In 1975, he was appointed District President of the Jana Sangh and nine years later, in 1984, he became the State President of the BJP youth wing. Four years later, in 1986, he became the National general secretary of the youth wing of the party and in 1988, the National President of the youth wing. In 1991, he became Education Minister in the first BJP government in the state of Uttar Pradesh and in 2000, was elected as the Chief Minister of the state. In 2003, he was made a cabinet minister in the NDA Government led by Mr Vajpayee. He served as the President of the BJP from 2005 to 2009, and was again elected as President in 2013, leading the party to victory in the 2014 general elections. Following this victory, he was appointed the Union Minister of Home Affairs in the NDA government led by Mr Narendra Modi and was sworn in on 26 May 2014.

S Jaishankar was appointed India's Foreign Secretary in January 2015. Born on January 9, 1955, he is an alumnus of Air Force Central School, New Delhi and St Stephen's College, Delhi. He has a Masters degree in Political Science and PhD in International Relations from Jawaharlal Nehru University (JNU), where he specialised in nuclear diplomacy. He joined Indian Foreign Service in 1977 and has served as India's Ambassador to the United States (2013–2015), China (2009–2013) and the Czech Republic (2001–04), and as High Commissioner to Singapore (2007–09). From 2004 to 2007, Jaishankar was Joint Secretary (Americas) at the Ministry of External Affairs in New Delhi. In this capacity, he was involved in negotiating the US-India civil nuclear agreement and improving defence co-operation, including during relief operations following the 2004 Indian Ocean tsunami. He was also involved with the conclusion of the 2005 New Defense Framework and the Open Skies Agreement, and he was associated with the launch of the US-India Energy Dialogue the India-US Economic Dialogue, and the India-US CEO's Forum. In 2006–2007, Jaishankar led the Indian team during the negotiations on the 123 Agreement with the United States.

Datuk Nur Jazlan Mohamed is a Malaysian politician and is the Member of the Parliament of Malaysia for the Pulai constituency in the state of Johor. He is a member of the United Malays National Organisation (UMNO) party in the governing Barisan Nasional coalition. On 28 July 2015, Nur Jazlan was elected as the Deputy Minister of Home Affairs.

Born on 15 February, 1966, Nur Jazlan is an alumnus from the South Bank Polytehnics, United Kingdom and Emile Woolf School of Accountancy, London. In 1990, he was appointed as one of the Administrative Executives in IGB Corporation Berhad. He stayed in IGB for a year before moving to Equatorial hotel (M) Sdn Bhd and later in 1994 he was appointed as the Finance Officer for the joint venture of Proton-DRB Sdn Bhd. He stayed there up till the year 2004, where he left his corporate life to contest in the 12th General Election, where he was elected to Federal Parliament in the 2004 election for the UMNO-held seat of Pulai and he retained his seat in the 2008 and 2013 elections. He is also a columnist for The Malaysian Insider.

Ajit Kumar Doval, KC is a former Indian intelligence and law enforcement officer, who, since 30 May 2014, is the 5th and current National Security Advisor to the Prime Minister of India. He had previously served as the Director of the Intelligence Bureau in 2004–05, after spending a decade as the head of its operations wing. Born in 1945 in Pauri Garhwal, he received his early education at the Ajmer Military School and later graduated with a master's degree in Economics from the University of Agra in 1967. He joined the IPS in 1968 in the Kerala cadre and was actively involved in anti-insurgency operations in Mizoram and Punjab. He was also one of three negotiators who negotiated the release of passengers from IC-814 in Kandahar in 1999. In Punjab, he was inside the Golden Temple in Amritsar in 1988 before Operation Black Thunder to collect critical information and was awarded the Kirti Chakra for conspicuous acts of bravery of a very high order. He retired in January 2005 as Director, Intelligence Bureau. In December 2009, he was the founder Director of the Vivekananda International Foundation, a think tank set up by the Vivekananda Kendra, a Spiritually Oriented Organisation and remained active in the discourse on national security in India, writing editorial pieces for several leading newspapers and journals and delivered lectures on India's security challenges and foreign policy objectives at several renowned government and non-governmental institutions, security think-tanks in India and abroad.

Amrullah Saleh was born in 1971 in the Panjshir Province of Afghanistan. He belongs to the Tajik group. In 1990, in order to avoid being conscripted into the Soviet-backed Afghan army, Saleh joined the opposition mujahideen forces. He received military training in Pakistan and fought under mujahideen commander Ahmad Shah Massoud. In the late 1990s, Saleh was a member of the Northern Alliance and fought against the Taliban expansion. In 1997, he was appointed by Massoud to lead the United Front's international liaison office at the Embassy of Afghanistan in Dushanbe, Tajikistan, where he served as a coordinator for non-governmental (humanitarian) organisations and as a liaison partner for foreign intelligence agencies. After the September 11, 2001 attacks in the United States, Saleh participated in leading intelligence operations of the United Front on the ground during the toppling of the Taliban regime. After the formation of the Islamic Republic of Afghanistan in December 2004, Saleh was appointed as head of the National Directorate of Security (NDS) by President Hamid Karzai. He initiated structural reforms and helped rebuild the Afghan intelligence service and was viewed by the international community as one of the most competent cabinet members in the Afghan government. He served as head of the National Directorate of Security from 2004 until his resignation in 2010, his resignation arising out of differences with President Karzai on how to proceed against the Taliban. Subsequently, in late 2010, Saleh created a pro-democracy and anti-Taliban movement called Basej-e Milli (National Mobilisation) and Green Trend, in which he remains actively engaged.

Md. Shahriar Alam, is the State Minister, Ministry of Foreign Affairs, Bangladesh. Born in 1970 in Chittagong, Mr. Alam received his Bachelor of Commerce Degree from City College, Dhaka and obtained an MBA from the Institute of Business Administration (IBA), University of Dhaka. Mr. Alam completed 1st CAPSTONE course at the National Defence College (NDC), Bangladesh. A successful businessman, with his main focus in textiles, Mr. Alam is deeply involved in politics and has been an active member of the Bangladesh Awami League since 1997. He has served as a Member of the Parliamentary Standing Committee in the Ministry of Science & Technology and acted as the Vice Chairman of All Party Parliamentary Group (APPG) on Climate Change, Education and Poverty Reduction and Vice Chairman of All party Parliamentary Group on MDGs, PRSP, WTO and Bangladesh Development Forum. He was elected a member of the National Parliament for the second consecutive term in January 2014, appointed to the Cabinet on 12 January 2014, and assumed charge as State Minister for Foreign Affairs on the same day. A widely travelled person, Mr. Alam is quite passionate about reading, music and sports, especially cricket, football, hockey, golf and lawn tennis.

Ibrahim Rahimpour, a career diplomat, is the Deputy Minister for Asia and Pacific Affairs in the Ministry of Foreign Affairs of Islamic

Republic of Iran since September 2013. He graduated in Economics from Sahid Beheshti University in 1977 and joined the Ministry of Foreign Affairs in 1981. He has held various important assignments in the Ministry. He was Iranian Charge de Affairs in Pakistan in 1984-85 and has been the Iranian Ambassador to India (1989-92), Austria (1998-2002) and Ireland (2008-2010).

P.C. Dogra is an ex. Indian Army Emergency Commission officer and later Punjab cadre I.P.S. officer. He fought Indo-Pak war of 1965 and led a company attack in the R.S. Pura sector of J&K. After his voluntary release from the army, he joined the I.P.S. After serving the state as Senior Superintendent of Police in various Districts, he went on deputation to CBI as D.I.G. When terrorism was at its peak, he was called back by the state and posted as D.I.G. of the sensitive ranges. Thereafter he also served as Inspector General of BSF-Jammu Frontier, IG/BSF Kashmir Frontier, IG/BSF Punjab Frontier. As Inspector General [Intelligence] at the BSF HQ, Delhi, he organised anti-militancy operations in J&K. In 1993, he was specifically picked up by the Ministry of Home Affairs, given adhoc promotion and posted as Additional Director General with a charge of Border Security Force units operating in J&K. On return to his state from deputation, he was posted as Director General of Police (Operations) Punjab. In 1997, he took over as Director General of Police of the state from where he retired in 1999. In 2003, he set up a "Forum on Integrated National Security" at Chandigarh. He has edited three books; *"Changing Perspective on National Security"*, *"Threat to Security. How Secure is India from within"* and *"Mumbai Siege. Enough is enough. Should it be our response?"* He is coming out with his own book titled *"Tribal Invasion of Kashmir. Analysing the role of Lord Mountbatten, Pt. Nehru, Sardar Patel, Maharaja Hari Singh and Sheikh Abdullah"*, an effort of a research work of the last ten years.

Manish Shanker Sharma is a senior IPS officer and currently serves as Inspector General of Police. He holds a Masters degree in International Affairs and Public Policy from the University of California, specialising in international security & counter terrorism. He has had a diverse experience of 24 years with the Government, having served across 4 continents. His background incorporates a unique composition of service in the fields of law enforcement, counter terrorism, diplomacy, UN peacekeeping in Europe and ensuring transportation security in India. Mr Sharma is also one of the very few experts in India who combine extensive international and national field level experience in combination with academic and scholarly work alongside outstanding international acclaim. He has served on various committees and panels of the Government of India and overseas. During his career, Mr. Sharma has been bestowed with a unique honour by the Mayor of San Diego, California who proclaimed July 20, 2015 as "Manish S. Sharma Day". He has also received Special Congressional Recognition of the US Congress for his services, the title of Honorary Mayor- President of the city of Baton Rouge and the United Nations Peace Medal among other honours.

Colonel Vivek Chadha is a research fellow at the Institute for Defence Studies and Analyses. He served in the Indian Army for 22 years before taking premature retirement. His research focus covers counter insurgency, counter terrorism and terrorism finance and he has written many articles on the above subjects. He also speaks extensively on the above issue in various establishments across the country. An erudite scholar, he has published a number of books, some of which are: *Lifeblood of Terrorism: Countering Terrorism Finance; Even If it Ain't Broke Yet Do Fix it: Enhancing Effectiveness Through Military Change; Low Intensity Conflict in India: An Analysis; Indo-US Relations: Divergence to Convergence; Company Commander in Low Intensity Conflict: Principles, Preparation and Conduct; Asian Strategic Review 2015: India as a Security Provider* (Ed); *Asian Strategic Review 2014: US Pivot and Asian Security* (Ed); *Asian Strategic Review* (Ed).

Amit Kumar is the President of AAA International Security Consultants LLC. Widely recognised as an international security expert in counterterrorism and counter-terrorist financing, Mr. Kumar is also a Senior Fellow with the Anti-Money Laundering Association (AMLA), an Adjunct Associate Professor at the Edmund A. Walsh School of Foreign Service at Georgetown University, a lecturer for the Graduate Certificate in Homeland Security Program at the Bush

School of Government & Public Service at Texas A&M University, and an International Associate with the Society for Policy Studies, New Delhi, India. Mr. Kumar till recently also served as the Fellow for Homeland Security and Counterterrorism at the Center for National Policy for several years. Mr. Kumar previously worked with the Al-Qaida Taliban Sanctions regime at the United Nations where he offered substantive advice to the Al-Qaida and Taliban Sanctions Regimes on matters related to the implementation of Assets Freeze Sanctions measures against the Al-Qaida and Taliban, as well as issues relating countering the financing of terrorism.

He earned a Doctorate in Public Administration from American University in Washington D.C.; a Masters in Philosophy in American Studies from the Jawaharlal Nehru University, New Delhi; and a Masters in International Business from the University of Delhi.

Lt. Col. (Res.) Uri Ben Yaakov is a Senior Researcher and Project Manager at The International Institute for Counter-Terrorism (ICT). He brings to ICT a wide experience in intelligence, analysis, research and management. He began his military service in the Paratroopers in the Israel Defense Forces (IDF) and continued his service in various intelligence positions. He has a BA in General Studies from Tel-Aviv University and later on completed his law studies. He finished his MA studies in Government with Specialisation in Counter-Terrorism & Homeland Security and a Certificate in Cyber-Terrorism from the Lauder School of Government, Diplomacy & Strategy at the Interdisciplinary Center (IDC) Herzliya. Lt. Col. (Res.) Ben Yaakov is an accomplished businessman with international experience in Europe, Israel and Asia. He is the representative of ICT to the Israeli Parliament for the proposed Counter-Terrorism Bill and a specialist in the field of Syria, Cyber-Terrorism, Terrorism Financing and International Cooperation.

Daniel Pipes, a historian, is the president of the Middle East Forum, an independent non-profit organisation. A former official in the U.S. departments of State and Defense, he has taught at the University of Chicago, Harvard, Pepperdine, and at the U.S. Naval War College.

Mr. Pipes has written sixteen books. His bi-weekly column is published in The Washington Times, National Review, and other publications. His current focus is on the political upheavals in the Middle East. He tweets at @DanielPipes.

His website, DanielPipes.org, with an archive of his writings and media appearances, has recorded 70 million page visits since its inception in 2000. More than 11,000 translations of his writings have been published in 37 languages.

Ajai Sahni is Founding Member & Executive Director of the Institute for Conflict Management; Editor, South Asia Intelligence Review; Executive Director, South Asia Terrorism Portal; Executive Editor, Faultlines: Writings on Conflict & Resolution. He has researched and written extensively on issues relating to conflict, politics and development in South Asia, and has participated in advisory projects undertaken for various National or State Governments. He jointly edited (with K.P.S. Gill) *Terror & Containment: Perspectives on India's Internal Security*; and *The Global Threat of Terror: Ideological, Material and Political Linkages*. He has lectured at numerous professional institutions, prominently including the National Defence College, Naval War College, College of Defence Management, Army War College, College of Air Warfare, ARTRAC, LBS National Academy of Administration, R&AW Training College, National Intelligence Academy and SVP National Police Academy, among others. He has appeared frequently as an expert on terrorism and insurgency in the electronic and print media in India and internationally.

Baker Atyani is Al Arabiya News Channel's bureau chief in South and East Asia. He is a veteran Jordanian journalist, covering conflict zones in Asia for the past 16 years and is an expert on militant groups in Asia. He has produced numerous documentaries, articles, and investigative stories and was the last journalist to interview Osama Bin Laden before 9/11. He has been honoured by MCF with "Exceptional Courage in Journalism" award. He had interviewed Osama bin Laden months before the Sept. 11 attacks. On June 5, 2012, he travelled to Manila to shoot two documentary films, including one on the living conditions of Muslims in the south of the Philippines. He was kidnapped by militant groups and held in the Sulu Islands in the Philippine province of Mindanao. After 18 months of captivity, Atyani, on December 4, 2013 became free after he managed to escape from his captors.

Lieutenant General K.T. Parnaik, PVSM, UYSM, YSM is an alumnus of the National Defence Academy, Khadakwasla, the Defence Service Staff College, Wellington and National Defence College, New Delhi. A third generation officer, he was commissioned in and commanded 2 Rajputana Rifles. The General has participated in the entire spectrum of counter insurgency operations in J&K and Northeast India. He was awarded Yudh Seva Medal for command of an active Brigade in J&K and Uttam Yudh Seva Medal for his assignment in a sensitive Corps in the North East. After a tenure as the Director General, Perspective Planning in Army Headquarters, responsible for Force Structuring and Modernisation of the Indian Army, he moved to Udhampur in January 01, 2011 to head the prestigious Northern Command as the Commander in Chief. For his outstanding leadership, strategic vision and effectively synergising the operators in J&K, he was awarded the Param Vishist Seva Medal in 2012. He has served abroad in UN Mission at Angola from 1997-99 as Chief of Staff and as the Commandant of Indian Military Training Team in Bhutan in 2007-08. Post retirement, the General is a regular speaker on defence and security issues in various military establishments, think tanks and Universities across India.

Sultan Shahin is an alumnus of Patna University and is the founder and editor of the multi-lingual Islamic website NewAgeIslam.com. His career in journalism spans 40 years during which time he has travelled extensively in India and abroad and has acquired expertise in Islamic theology, politics, and culture as well as an empirical knowledge of the impact of religion and ideology over radicalisation and radicalism. He has written edit-page articles, opinion pieces, special reports, and columns for major Indian publications such as the Hindustan Times, The Indian Express, The Times of India, The Asian Age, etc. as well as for international newspapers such as the Asia Times Online, Hong Kong. His website is aimed at engaging with the Muslim communities across the world, to encourage open debate and to rethink Islam by fighting xenophobia, religious intolerance and gender inequality in Islamic societies. Its main focus is to combat jihadi radicalism at an ideological level by promoting a progressive interpretation of the Islamic scriptures.

Lisa Curtis is Senior Research Fellow for South Asia in the Asian Studies Center at the Heritage Foundation. Since joining Heritage in August 2006, Curtis has appeared on major broadcast networks, including CNN, Fox News, PBS, and BBC, to comment on developments in South Asia and testified over a dozen times before Congress on issues related to U.S. policy toward India, Pakistan, and Afghanistan. Her commentary has appeared in The Los Angeles Times, U.S. News and World Report, Foreign Policy, and The National Interest, and in South Asian publications such as The Hindu, India Today, The Friday Times, The News, and Express Tribune. Before joining Heritage, she was Professional Staff Member of the Senate Foreign Relations Committee, handling the South Asia portfolio for then Committee Chairman, Senator Richard Lugar (R-IN). From 2001 to 2003, Curtis served as Senior Advisor in the State Department's South Asia Bureau, where she advised the Assistant Secretary on India-Pakistan relations. In the late 1990s, Curtis served in the Central Intelligence Agency as a political analyst on South Asia. She also served as a political officer to the U.S. embassies in Islamabad and in New Delhi from 1994 to 1998.

Christian Wagner specialises on issues relating to Foreign Policy and Security in South Asia, Regional Cooperation, Democracy and Ethnic Conflicts in South Asia. He received his Masters degree in Political Science from Freiburg University and obtained his Doctor of Philosophy degree from Habilitation, University of Rostock. He has served as Lecturer in the Department of Political Science, University of Freiburg, Administrative Officer at University of Mainz, Research Fellow at the Center for Modern Oriental Studies, Berlin, Assistant Professor at the Institute for Political Science and Administrative Studies, University of Rostock, Senior Research Fellow at the Center for Development Research at University of Bonn and Visiting Fellow at IDSA, New Delhi. His publications include 'The Effects of the

China-Pakistan Economic Corridor on India-Pakistan Relations', 'The Role of India and China in South Asia' and 'Security Cooperation in South Asia', amongst others.

Admiral (Dr.) Jayanath Colombage is an alumnus of the Defence Services Staff College, Wellington in India, Asia Pacific Center for Security Studies, Hawaii in the United States and Royal College of Defence Studies in the United Kingdom. He joined the Sri Lanka Navy as an Officer Cadet in 1978 and successfully completed his basic training at the renowned Naval and Maritime Academy in Trincomalee, winning the 'Sword of Honour' for the Best Officer Cadet of the 7th Intake. Admiral Colombage has commanded numerous ships of the Sri Lanka Navy including the Fast Missile Vessels, Fast Gun Boats, Fast Attack Craft and amphibious ships and has been awarded the Surface Warfare Badge. He is a weapon specialist who has undergone extensive training with the Indian Navy and in the People's Republic of China. He has commanded four Operational Naval Commands, namely, Eastern, Northern, Western and North Central, for a period of over 5 years. After command of the Eastern Naval Area, he was appointed to the highest seat of Commander of the Sri Lanka Navy, where he served from 2012 -2014. A recipient of the Rana Sura Padakkama for gallantry, Admiral Colambage is also an erudite scholar. He has published a book titled 'Naval Terms and Expressions' and actively contributes to various academic forums.

Index